Exploring British Sign Language via Systemic Functional Linguistics

Bloomsbury Studies in Systemic Functional Linguistics

Series Editors: J. R. Martin, John Knox and David Caldwell

Among functional approaches to language and related semiotic systems, Systemic Functional theory stands out as an evolving paradigm, constantly developing new systems to accommodate descriptive challenges. Bloomsbury Studies in Systemic Functional Linguistics responds to this ever-developing field, speaking to instances of evolution at the frontier of the discipline.

Publishing contemporary, cutting-edge research in Systemic Functional Linguistics, this cohesive series unites complementary developments into an integrated multiperspectival whole. Titles focus on specific themes to explore emerging new fields of research in Systemic Functional theory alongside innovations within long established areas of SFL research. Placing emphasis on new voices and directions, Bloomsbury Studies in Systemic Functional Linguistics demonstrates how a disciplinary singular like SFL continues to evolve and subsume its past into possible futures.

Upcoming titles in the series:

Modelling Paralanguage Using Systemic Functional Semiotics: Theory and Application, edited by Thu Ngo, Susan Hood, J. R. Martin, Clare Painter, Bradley A. Smith, Michele Zappavigna
Interpersonal Meaning in Multimodal English Textbooks, by Yumin Chen
Appliable Linguistics and Social Semiotics, edited by J. R. Martin, John Knox, David Caldwell

Exploring British Sign Language via Systemic Functional Linguistics

A Metafunctional Approach

Luke A. Rudge

BLOOMSBURY ACADEMIC
LONDON • NEW YORK • OXFORD • NEW DELHI • SYDNEY

BLOOMSBURY ACADEMIC
Bloomsbury Publishing Plc
50 Bedford Square, London, WC1B 3DP, UK
1385 Broadway, New York, NY 10018, USA
29 Earlsfort Terrace, Dublin 2, Ireland

BLOOMSBURY, BLOOMSBURY ACADEMIC and the Diana logo are
trademarks of Bloomsbury Publishing Plc

First published in Great Britain 2022
Paperback edition published 2024
Copyright © Luke A. Rudge, 2022

A catalogue record for this book is available from the British Library.

A catalog record for this book is available from the Library of Congress.

ISBN: HB: 978-1-3501-4894-9
PB: 978-1-3503-3430-4
ePDF: 978-1-3501-4895-6
eBook: 978-1-3501-4896-3

Series: Bloomsbury Studies in Systemic Functional Linguistics

Typeset by Integra Software Services Pvt. Ltd.

To find out more about our authors and books visit www.bloomsbury.com
and sign up for our newsletters.

Contents

Figures

Tables

Acknowledgements

'Language itself is not designed to conform to our models so there will always be instances that will perplex even the best one' (Fontaine, 2013, p.217). This was the final citation of my doctoral thesis (Rudge, 2018), which presented the first description and analysis of a sign language – specifically, British Sign Language (BSL) – from the perspective of Systemic Functional Linguistics (SFL). Since completing my PhD, I have had the chance to explore the visual-spatial modality in far more detail, which has greatly assisted in the creation of the present work. However, the above quote continues to be true: no matter how robust a box you may create to contain a language, it will always find a way to burst the boundaries.

Fontaine's (2013) quote is used here for two reasons. Not only does it succinctly summarize the intrigue, challenge and ire felt by linguists the world over, but it also feels suitable to dedicate the first quote in this book to Lise Fontaine. Lise was an external examiner for my Viva Voce examination, and also the first linguist from the systemic functional domain who reached out to me, to invite me to an SFL event at Cardiff University in the early stages of my doctoral research. From those early interactions, I went on to meet hundreds of other systemic functional linguists – from Early Career Researchers all the way through to those who had worked for decades with M. A. K. Halliday, Ruqaiya Hasan and other giants in the field. I have been offered many opportunities to take part in scholarly activities with this supportive community, including the creation of this book. There are far too many people to name, but this small dedication goes towards those who make this community such a pleasure to be a part of.

My thanks also extend to many others: to my colleagues and students in the Bristol Centre for Linguistics for being an absolute joy to work with; to my mother, father and family near and far for their unwavering encouragement and support; to the editors of this series for their expert guidance; and to the deaf community for teaching me so much about BSL and deaf cultures.

Last, but by no means least, my greatest thanks go to David. Words on a page will never be enough to express my gratitude for your seemingly endless supply of support, time and love. Here's to many more adventures and shenanigans together!

Abbreviations

ASL	American Sign Language
Auslan	Australian Sign Language
BANZSL	British, Australian and New Zealand Sign Language
BSL	British Sign Language
CLU	Clause-like unit
DGS	Deutsche Gebärdensprache (German Sign Language)
ELAN	The EUDICO Linguistic Annotator
FinSL	Suomalainen Viittomakieli (Finnish Sign Language)
HamNoSys	The Hamburg Notation System
IPSL	Indo-Pakistani Sign Language
LSC	Llengua de signes catalana (Catalan Sign Language)
LSFB	Langue des signes de Belgique francophone (French Belgian Sign Language)
NGT	Nederlandse Gebarentaal (Sign Language of the Netherlands)
NSL	Norsk Tegnspråk (Norwegian Sign Language)
NZSL	New Zealand Sign Language
RRG	Role and Reference Grammar
SFL	Systemic Functional Linguistics

1

Introducing British Sign Language:
A Sociocultural and Linguistic Overview

Languages and their sociocultural contexts of use are tightly intertwined. Influence is constantly exerted between them, alongside external influences, such that the use of a language entails playing a part in its associated culture(s) in some way. In a similar vein, to understand a language, there must be an understanding of its cultural context and place in the world.

Before diving into any deep linguistic description, it is necessary to begin with an introduction to British Sign Language (BSL) from a sociocultural perspective. I aim to provide the reader with a deeper awareness with regard to the language, its users, the cultural labels that are used and the development of BSL, ranging from several centuries ago through to contemporary events and legislation enacted within the UK. The focus then shifts towards broad linguistic aspects of BSL, presenting an overview of some of the core elements of BSL production. This linguistic summary acts as a primer to the following chapters, wherein BSL is observed, described and analysed through the lens of Systemic Functional Linguistics (SFL).

If readers are neither BSL users nor users of another sign language, the second half of this chapter offers a useful base from which further linguistic discussion can grow, and as a point of reference for terms and concepts that are revisited throughout later chapters. It must be noted that what is offered in this chapter is by no means a complete introduction to BSL and that the most appropriate way to become engaged with BSL (or any sign language) is to attend registered, deaf-led classes. Nonetheless, this initial introduction suffices as an introductory exploration of the language, and concepts that may require further clarification will be elaborated on where required.

A sociocultural overview of British Sign Language

'Deaf' or 'deaf?'

When speaking of a culture and its development, an appropriate label or descriptor must be employed. The terminological appropriacy of referring to deaf people and wider deaf communities has been discussed in depth, and many terms have been proposed and deployed over decades of deaf studies and sign language research. However, it must be borne in mind that not all sign language users may identify as culturally and/or audiologically deaf, just as those who identify as deaf may not wish to use a sign language as a primary method of communication.

Various terms have been proposed over several decades, including 'sign language peoples' (Batterbury, 2012; Batterbury, Ladd and Gulliver, 2007) and 'people of the eye' (McKee, 2001), but a more lasting distinction follows Woodward's (1975) uppercase and lowercase dichotomy (i.e. 'Deaf' and 'deaf'). The former refers to a group 'who do not identify with the wider (dominant) society based on their hearing status' (Napier and Leeson, 2016, p.21), whereas the latter refers to those who do not identify as part of a deaf community and who may prefer to use a spoken language as a primary method of communication.

I have employed this dichotomy in previous work (e.g. Rudge, 2018). However, as the world moves towards a greater recognition of intersectionality, various scholars (e.g. Kusters, De Meulder and O'Brien, 2017) are moving away from this dichotomy, as it is deemed 'an oversimplification of what is an increasingly complex set of identities and language practices, which are impossible to represent with a simplified binary' (De Meulder, Murray and McKee, 2019, p.40). As used by De Meulder, Murray and McKee (2019), and for the sake of brevity within the wider aims of this work, I will deploy the lowercase 'deaf' usage. This is done with the caveat that it is chosen without the intention to reduce a complex sociocultural construction to a one-dimensional term.

Tracing the origins of BSL

Sign languages operate in the visual-spatial modality for linguistic production and reception. As such, to capture and preserve interactions using sign languages, access to appropriate recording devices is essential. At the time of writing, the number of image capture devices that are accessible to the public is remarkable: combining the ubiquity of access to devices such as modern smartphones with ever-increasing digital storage capacities and speeds of data transmission, there is no issue when it comes to almost instantaneous recording and preservation of visual data. However, even as recently as the early 2000s, such technology did not permit such ease of visual capture, in terms of both quality and accessibility. Going only a few more decades back results in a very different landscape – one in which video data recording and storage was expensive, bulky and generally reserved for more specialist contexts. It is therefore understandable that the rapid development of image capture technology has had significant impacts on our knowledge of sign languages.

Various online resources are available that trace the cultural history of BSL and its users, such as the websites for the British Deaf Association,[1] the British Deaf History Society[2] and University College London's presentations of BSL history.[3] In combination with scholarly works such as Jackson (2001) and Ladd (2003), the task of presenting the history and development of sign languages is not as tricky as it could be, although many gaps in knowledge still exist. Based on the resources noted above, it has been proposed that the use of communication systems akin to sign languages can be traced as far back as 422 BC. The first documented use of a sign language in Britain was noted to occur in February 1576, as documented in a marriage record from St Martin's Church in Leicester (wherein it is explained that proceedings occurred via embodied communication in lieu of speech). Records also indicate that the first British school for the Deaf was established by Thomas Braidwood in Edinburgh in 1760. As Jackson (2001) notes, 'unless it is written about in other people's writings or preserved in art form, no record exists' (p.25). Nonetheless, despite sparse evidence, it can be ascertained from these details that sign languages are by no means a novel aspect of communication overall. They have existed and developed in various forms over many centuries.

The rise and fall of Oralism

In 1880, a significant event occurred that had a severe and detrimental impact on the recognition and development of sign languages around the world. Oralism, or 'the oral method' – 'an all-encompassing set of policies and discourses aimed at preventing [deaf communities] from learning or using sign languages to communicate' (Ladd, 2003, p.7) – was presented during the Second International Congress of Instructors of the Deaf and Dumb in Milan. Through a combination of flawed argumentation, misrepresentation and bias, oralism was promoted as the most suitable way to teach deaf children, rather than using a sign language alongside speech and/or writing. This decision resulted in the prohibition of sign language use in classroom instruction and, through various sociocultural pressures, its repression in multiple other aspects of daily life. Kendon (2004) identifies the arguments that were presented to promote the use of oralism, such as 'if the deaf could be taught to speak they could much more easily fit in with everyday life' (p.64). Furthermore, the use of sign language was deemed 'the root cause of perpetuating a lower class leading to stigmatisation' (Jackson, 2001, p.33), and sign languages overall were viewed 'as a last option for those considered "not intelligent enough" to speak' (Napier and Leeson, 2016, p.75). Sicard (1984) harrowingly exemplifies the resulting hostility towards deaf communities during this era, noting that a deaf person was viewed as:

> a mere ambulatory machine whose constitution (as regards his behaviour) is inferior to that of animals. In saying that he is primitive, we are still underestimating his pitifulness, for he is not even the equal of primitive man in morality or in communication.
>
> (p.85)

Oralism became deeply entrenched for decades. However, the work of Tervoort (1953) on Nederlandse Gebarentaal (NGT; Sign Language of the Netherlands) and Stokoe (1960) on American Sign Language (ASL) was crucial in what would be the turning point to this misguided, misinformed and often dangerous approach. These two works heralded the start of modern sign linguistics studies, with a meeting of the International Congress on the Education of the Deaf held in Manchester in 1985 being a vital first step in the start of studies for BSL (Jackson, 2001). Though sign linguistics and deaf studies have grown rapidly since this time and methods of instruction in deaf classrooms have improved considerably in recent decades, oralist attitudes do sadly resurface (see, e.g., Rathkey, 2019). Much work remains to undo the subsequent effects of decisions made over a century ago.

BSL in the twenty-first century

Nearly one-quarter of the way into the twenty-first century, the state of BSL paints a curious picture (elaborated and discussed further in works such as Lawson et al., 2019). Firstly, a question surrounding the number of BSL users arises, which ends up being an extremely challenging figure to determine. Looking back a decade or so, the UK Census of 2011 (Office for National Statistics, 2013) estimated 15,000 BSL users in the UK. Yet, more recently, the British Deaf Association (2019) has estimated 151,000 BSL users in the UK, of which 87,000 identify as deaf. This latter figure matches the Royal Association for Deaf People's (2020) estimate of 87,000, but this figure refers to the total number of BSL users in the UK *regardless* of their deaf or hearing identity. From academic perspectives, too, the figures do not seem to align. Napier and Leeson (2016), for example, state that '250,000 use BSL daily in the UK, 70,000 of whom are deaf' (p.54). This variation may be attributed to multiple factors, such as inadequate survey methodologies, the perceived sociocultural values of identifying as a BSL user and the impact that the inclusion of sign languages in national and international legislation might have on such perceptions (see, e.g., Caudrelier, 2014, for further elaboration).

The area of linguistic recognition and legislation may be further scrutinized. In 2003, BSL gained the status of an official minority language in the UK, and the BSL (Scotland) Act received Royal Assent in late 2015. Despite this, government support for the use of and access to BSL is sparse, particularly when considered alongside other minority languages in the UK that have received significant financial and institutional support (e.g. Welsh; see Lawson et al., 2019 for further exemplification of the disregard towards BSL recognition at legislative levels). This seeming indifference has been witnessed of late within England during the preliminary stages of the Covid-19 pandemic in 2020. Daily televised briefings from Downing Street were presented with critical information in spoken English, yet without BSL interpretation. This led to the creation of the 'Where Is the Interpreter?' campaign led by deaf activist Lynn Stewart-Taylor, who continues to fight for legal action over the lack of BSL interpretation and access for deaf people at key events, such as the 2021 United Nations Climate Change Conference (COP26; see Centre for Deaf and Hard of Hearing People, 2020; Stewart-Taylor, 2021).

From educational perspectives, specialist provision of resources for deaf children has dropped dramatically over recent decades. Moore (2008) identified seventy-five schools for the deaf operating in the UK in 1982. A more recent survey by the Consortium for Research into Deaf Education (CRIDE, 2018) now estimates that 52,000 deaf children in the UK are served by only nineteen institutions with school-based provision, of which just nine are classed as a 'special school for deaf children' (p.11). Provision for the study of BSL and tangential subjects (e.g. deaf studies and sign language interpretation) in Higher Education is also low. At the time of writing, the Universities and Colleges Admissions Service[4] presents fewer than fifty programmes of study by sixteen providers, both at undergraduate and postgraduate levels.

Nevertheless, research into sign languages continues to grow in academic and community contexts, as does the number of international conferences that either address sign languages and deaf studies specifically, or that offer sessions concerning these areas. This research is gradually expanding into newer fields (as exemplified by the work presented in this book). Additionally, the tone of recognition and legitimacy of these studies in contemporary terms now starkly contrasts that which was noted in previous decades (see Sicard, 1984). It is now common to find statements like the following by Dachkovsky, Healy and Sandler (2013):

> sign languages seem to function just like spoken languages, are acquired by children just as automatically and on the same timetable as spoken languages [...], have much neurological overlap [...] and emerge spontaneously whenever a community of deaf people has an opportunity to form.
>
> (p.244)

As a research community, we are now in a position of knowing more about BSL from numerous perspectives. Calling on knowledge of historical events and language evolution, we can understand why BSL, Australian Sign Language (Auslan) and New Zealand Sign Language (NZSL) display such productive similarities despite their geographical distance (see Johnston, 2003, who argues for all three to be viewed as varieties of one larger sign language: BANZSL). More locally, we can document and investigate the regional variation found in BSL across the UK, including but is not limited to signs used for colours, numbers and place names (Quinn, 2010; Stamp et al., 2014, 2015). This work is facilitated by ongoing technological developments that permit us to work with digital Signbanks that can be accessed by academics and the public alike.[5] However, with new advances come new challenges, such as accurate and consistent transcription and annotation (Cormier et al., 2017) and questions surrounding the lemmatization of signs (Fenlon, Cormier and Schembri, 2015). All this work is undertaken with the agreed acknowledgement that BSL and other sign languages have 'no standard form or ultimate authority to which one can appeal for judgments of "correctness"' (Sutton-Spence, 1999, p.365) and that many sign languages exist 'without well-developed community-based standards of correctness' (Napoli and Sutton-Spence, 2014, p.2).

This brief exposition of the history and of the continued ups and downs of sign language use and study (and of BSL in particular) has intended to demonstrate that there are many sociocultural aspects that need to be borne in mind when approaching studies in this area. As noted at the start of this chapter, a language and its culture are closely intertwined, so knowledge and acknowledgement of the latter are important before exploring the former. Space limits the amount of discussion that can be included here regarding these topics. Nonetheless, readers are encouraged to refer to the further literature available within this domain, particularly those authored by members of the deaf community (e.g. Ladd, 2003).

A linguistic overview of BSL

The expression of BSL is located in the visual-spatial modality. Through combinations of embodied articulators – the hands, eyebrows, torso and mouth, to name a few – within an area in front of a signer known as the signing space, linguistic meanings are made. Although visual in its nature, BSL is not complemented by a writing system in a similar way that, for instance, spoken English is complemented by written English. The writing systems that have been developed to transcribe BSL and other sign languages are mainly taken up for analytical/academic purposes. This includes systems such as Stokoe Notation, the Berkeley Transcription System (Slobin et al., 2001), the Hamburg Notation System (Hanke, 2004) and the Typannot Approach (Bianchini et al., 2018).

The second part of this chapter provides an overview of the productive components of BSL, although it must be borne in mind that this is not intended to be a complete introduction to the linguistics of BSL. Many other publications fulfil this role for BSL and other sign languages (e.g. Baker et al., 2016; Sutton-Spence and Woll, 1999). The following overview has been organized to allow a non-signer to understand the descriptions and analyses that they will encounter throughout this work.

Making use of the hands

The hands have the potential to display multiple configurations in their form. From gestural and sign language perspectives, variations in these forms lead to variations in meaning, thereby suggesting several phonological parameters that may be identified (Orfanidou et al., 2009).[6] These parameters are *handshape, orientation, location* and *movement*. These are overviewed here, and more detailed information on each parameter is offered by Van der Kooij and Crasborn (2016).

Handshape concerns the configuration of the fingers on a signer's hands: fingers may be 'selected' (i.e. extended) to differing extents and in various combinations. For instance, the index finger may be selected in isolation and extended straight out, while the other fingers remain in a 'non-selected' position (i.e. tucked into the palm). Fingers may also bend at the joints to give curved or clawed shapes. When more than one finger is selected, further variables include how spaced out the fingers are (e.g. in contact or spread apart) and whether the handshape is open (palm visible) or closed (palm covered).

Orientation involves the palms of the hand. In brief, it is the direction in which the palms are facing relative to the physical context and/or to one another. For example, a flat handshape (i.e. with all fingers selected and with no spacing between the fingers) in a typically 'offering' gesture will have a palm-upwards (supine) orientation.

Location concerns the position of the hands in relation to the signer as a sign is produced. A sign may be located in a neutral space (i.e. the space in front of the signer) or in a more specific area around the upper body: the forehead, the temples, the neck, the chest, the arms, to name a few. Each of these may also include contact with the body part in question.

Finally, movement may be divided into two sub-categories: hand-internal movement (i.e. movement of the selected fingers at the joints) or path movement (i.e. movement of the whole hand through the signing space). While a sign may include both hand-internal movement and path movement, phonotactic restrictions exist such as the Selected Fingers Constraint (Mandel, 1981; Sandler and Lillo-Martin, 2006). For example, a hand-internal movement can modify the curvature, spacing or 'openness' of a handshape either once or in a repeated fashion, but this movement cannot result in the deselection of some fingers followed by the selection of other fingers. So, a repetition of a full extension of the index and middle fingers, then retracting them while fully extending the thumb and little finger, would be in breach of the Selected Fingers Constraint.

To demonstrate what these four phonological parameters look like in practice, Figure 1.1 illustrates two signs in BSL and their respective values.

Making use of the upper body

Other embodied features also contribute to meaning making in BSL, beyond the four manual phonological parameters discussed above. These non-manual parameters include the head, the face and its various sub-features, the shoulders and the torso.

Sign	ELEVEN	DISAPPOINT
Handshape	Index finger selected	Index and middle; spread
Orientation	Palm away from signer	Palm down
Location	Neutral space	Neck (contacting)
Movement	Internal (repeated flexion)	None

Figure 1.1 The phonological parameters of ELEVEN and DISAPPOINT.

Head movements can be broad or nuanced, from a vigorous headshake suggesting a strong level of objection, to a small tilt to the left or right when posing a question. Various articulators on the face can move with precision and combine in several ways. Working down from the top of the face, the first primary articulators are the eyebrows. Their positions – raised, neutral or furrowed – can provide important distinctions in linguistic interaction, such as the difference between a statement and a question (as will be discussed in Chapter 3). The next articulators further down on the face, the eyes, can be altered in terms of aperture (e.g. wide, neutral, narrowed and closed) and gaze direction – the functions of which are still a matter of discussion between numerous sign linguists (see, *inter alia*, Cormier, Smith and Sevcikova-Sehyr, 2015; Ferrara, 2019; Neidle et al., 2000; Sandler and Lillo-Martin, 2006). Finally, the mouth as articulator can be split into two broad functions: mouthing and mouth gesture (Lewin and Schembri, 2011). In short, mouthing in BSL is the 'silent spoken production' of a sign's equivalent English word as the sign is manually produced (such as signing MOTHER and producing *mum* on the lips). Mouth gestures, however, are used to add further information, such as adverbial or circumstantial dimensions for the actions being expressed.

These facial features act in tandem, and different combinations lead to different meanings being made. A selection of these and how they may be used in BSL can be seen in Figure 1.2.

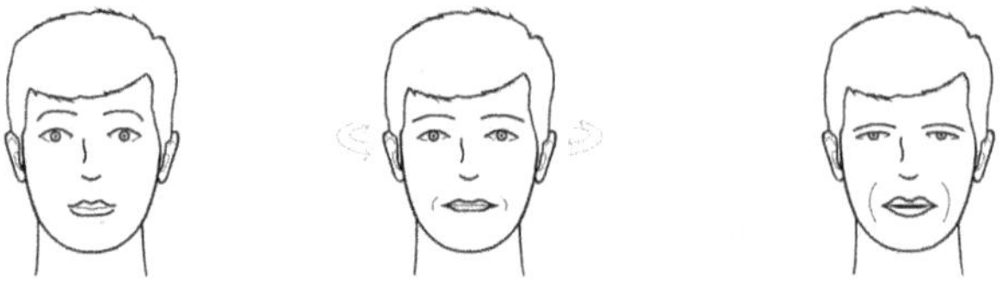

	Questioning	Negating	Expressing 'big,' 'expansive,' etc.
Head	Neutral or slight tilt	Repeated twist left to right	Neutral
Eyebrows	Raised	Neutral	Furrowed
Eye aperture	Wide	Neutral	Narrow
Mouth	Neutral	Stretched lips	Puffed-out lips and cheeks

Figure 1.2 Facial features and possible meanings conveyed in BSL.

Finally, the shoulders, chest and torso can alter in a similar way to the head, including tilting, twisting and leaning. These broader movements accompany the other non-manual features noted above, particularly when the signer is portraying the actions or dialogue of someone else (discussed in more detail in the following sections). For instance, a signer facing an interlocutor directly may twist their head, shoulders and torso to the left or right during an interaction to indicate that the signer has moved from 'narration' mode (i.e. signing as themselves) to 'reporting' mode (i.e. signing as someone or something else). This is also known as role shift or referential shift (see, e.g., Earis and Cormier, 2013).

Making use of space, sequentially and simultaneously

The signing space is the three-dimensional area in which a signer's hands typically move and interact. As suggested by Figure 1.3, this space extends vertically from just above the head to just below the torso, and extends horizontally and away from the signer. As such, the hands can move in this space without the need for overextension of the arms.

The signing space is significant in a multitude of ways, a sample of which will be presented here. Firstly, the signing space can be used to reference or 'place' elements that are being signed about. A signer may, for instance, express a specific person either by fingerspelling their name (e.g. -d-a-v-i-d-) or by producing the person's sign name.[7] Then, the signer can point to a position within the signing space to 'place' that person which can be referred to anaphorically in the discourse, either by pointing to that location again or by using certain signs that involve movement to or from that location. Depending on the information

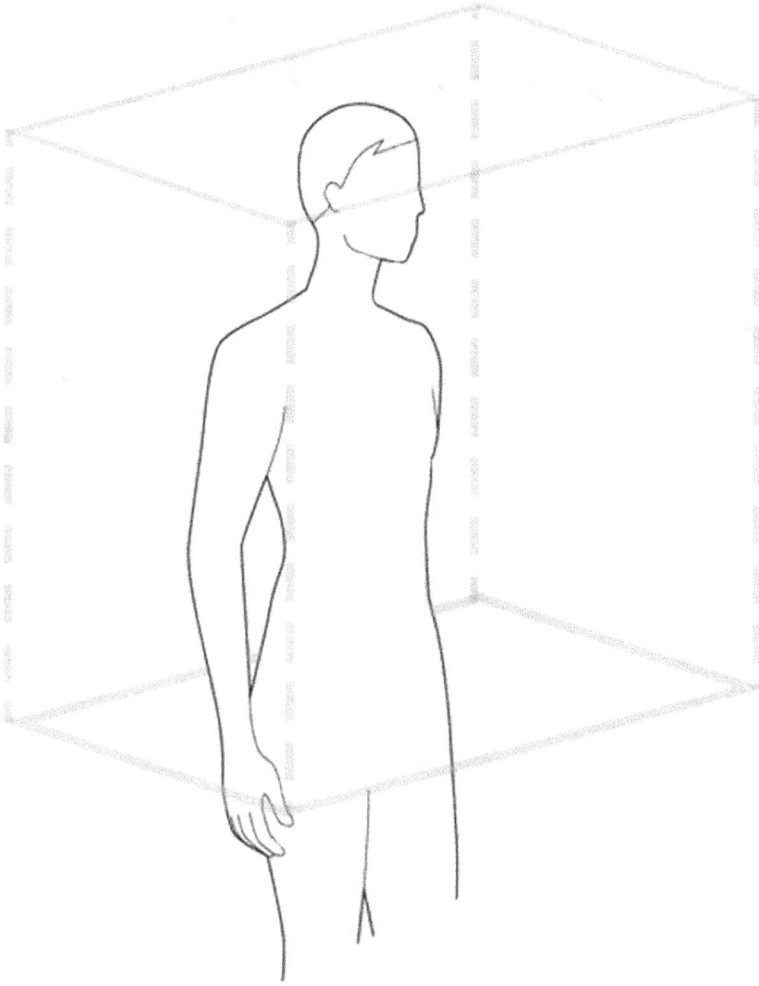

Figure 1.3 A basic model of the signing space.

produced in the utterance, the space may be interpreted as topographic (if creating an imagined physical space) or arbitrary (if assigning referents to fulfil grammatical roles; see Cormier, Fenlon and Schembri, 2015).

Secondly, the speed with which signs move in the signing space can alter the intended meaning. For example, READ can be expressed through a zig-zag motion of the signer's dominant hand (which takes a form representing a reader's gaze) in front of the palm of the non-dominant hand (which takes a form representing the thing being read; see Figure 1.4). The movement of the

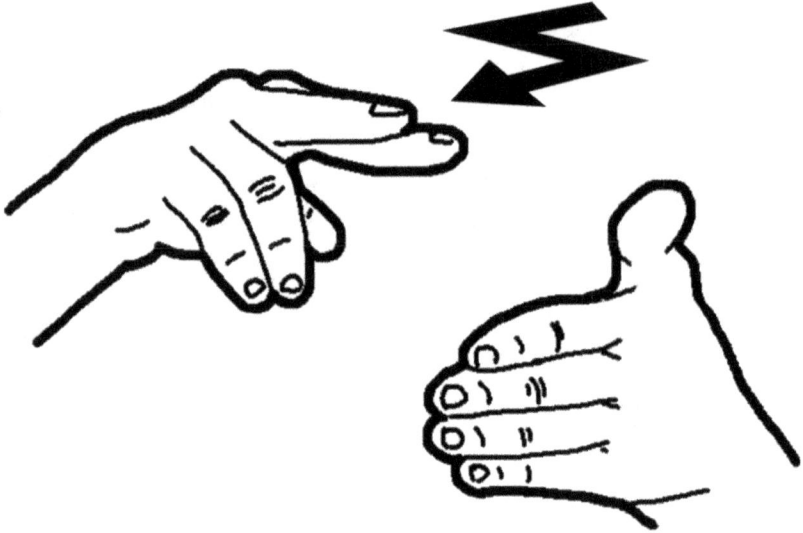

Figure 1.4 READ in BSL.

dominant hand could be produced with a quicker motion, expressing a meaning akin to READ-QUICKLY or SKIM. Or, it could be produced with a slower or more elaborate motion, expressing a meaning akin to READ-SLOWLY or READ-CLOSELY. The speed of a sign may also increase or decrease over a period of time: SKIM can become READ-CLOSELY, for instance, by the deceleration of the path movement of the dominant hand.

Thirdly, the locations of, and interactions between, the hands and referents placed in the signing space can also impact the meaning. When the signing space is used topographically, the hands may represent physical objects in an imagined space. Factors such as their location in relation to one another, and any interactions that occur between them, will therefore be meaning bearing. A simple example involves the use of a flat handshape to represent a flat object, such as a sheet of paper. Figure 1.5 demonstrates how two such handshapes can be used in the signing space, with changes in location and interaction leading to parallel changes in meaning.

At this point, it is clear that BSL is more than what is produced on the hands. There are a multitude of parameters found in the manual, non-manual and spatio-kinetic elements of signed production that must be observed in combination to understand the meanings being produced. As will be exemplified in later chapters, these elements may change one after another, some may persist as others change (i.e. the suprasegmental use of non-manual features as manual

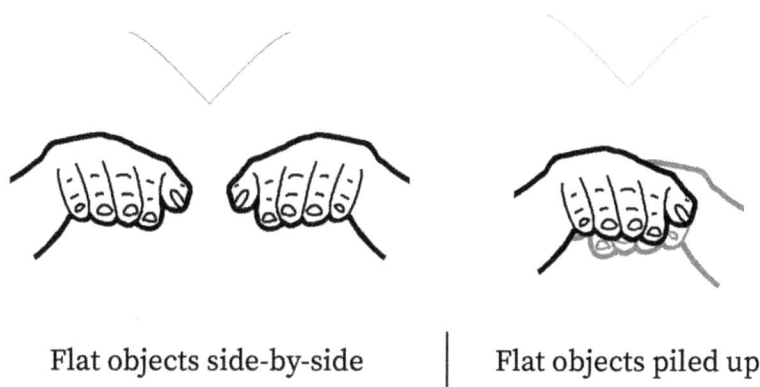

Flat objects side-by-side | Flat objects piled up

Figure 1.5 Differences in hand position leading to differences in meaning.

signs continue to change) and some may produce two distinct yet related meanings at the same point in time (i.e. 'simultaneous signs'). To contextualize these possibilities further before drawing the chapter to a close, it is worth summarizing a categorical distinction that has been made in sign language studies regarding sign types.

Types of signs and of signing

In BSL, and in many other sign languages in the world, a general categorization of signs may be employed according to their lexical status. Drawing on Hodge and Johnson's (2014) work on Auslan, signs in BSL may be fully or partly lexical – a division that will be useful to bear in mind in later chapters.[8]

Fully lexical signs form the listable core lexicon of a sign language (Sutton-Spence and Woll, 1999) and lend themselves to a definition in a dictionary (Brien, 1992; Fenlon et al., 2014a). These are the signs that 'generally align with prototypical notions of words in [spoken languages]' (Hodge and Johnston, 2014, p.267), and are generally expressed as a combination of manual phonological parameters with mouthing or mouth gestures. Two examples of fully lexical signs in BSL – ELEVEN and DISAPPOINT – were presented in Figure 1.1. When combined with other non-manual elements, additional meaning can be produced (e.g. DISAPPOINT with a downturned mouth and furrowed eyebrows can indicate a greater degree of disappointment or VERY-DISAPPOINTED).

Partly lexical signs, however, have only some conventional aspects and cannot easily be presented in a listable format. In these cases, certain manual parameters such as handshape can be used to represent a previously expressed concept (e.g. an (in)animate object or the manner of handling an object; see Cormier et al., 2012) which may then be combined with further manual, non-manual and spatio-kinetic elements to produce a complete meaning. An example of partly lexical signs was presented in Figure 1.5, wherein two flat handshapes represented individual flat objects. To complete the meaning, it is necessary to understand what they are representing (e.g. two pieces of paper) and their relative locations in the topographic signing space. These instances are called depicting constructions, although other terms exist such as classifier constructions (Emmorey, 2003). Pointing signs may also be classed as partly lexical as 'they have partly conventional aspects and index something in the signing space' (Hodge and Johnston, 2014, p.267).

Summary and book structure

At the start of this chapter, I argued that a language and its sociocultural context are closely intertwined. It is hoped at this point that readers will have a greater understanding of why this proposal was entertained, as well as a greater knowledge of BSL, its context and the context of its users. It would have been simple to write only the second half of this chapter, given the primarily linguistic nature of this work. To have done so, though, would have been to perform a great disservice to BSL and its users. It is not possible to understand a language in sufficient depth if its sociocultural dimensions are set aside, and even a general introduction to these dimensions can enable a richer understanding of the task at hand. As such, this introductory chapter has intended to serve as a primer from the perspectives of both BSL and the culture it encodes.

Similarly, it is hoped that the brief linguistic overview of BSL has disabused readers of preconceptions regarding the linguistic status of BSL. Like other sign languages of the world, BSL is just as rich linguistically speaking as spoken and written languages. Its meaning potential will be elaborated through description and analysis in the remainder of this work as follows. In Chapter 2, the field of SFL will be introduced and explained, permitting readers outside of this field to gain an understanding of its core 'facets'. I then move on to the initial considerations that must be borne in mind when attempting to use SFL to create a sufficiently detailed linguistic description of a visual-spatial language. In Chapters 3, 4 and 5,

BSL is explored, described and analysed in-depth through three metafunctional lenses: the interpersonal, experiential and textual, respectively. Each of these metafunctions presents a core aspect of meaning that can be made using semiotic systems. This includes how 'moves' are made between BSL users when giving or requesting information, how aspects of experience can be encoded in BSL and how the organization of signs into a sequence can lead to the highlighting or heightened prominence of certain parts over others. At the end of each of these chapters, a full 'system network' details how selections in meaning can be made in BSL, accompanied by 'realization statements' which demonstrate how this meaning is realized lexicogrammatically in BSL. Following this, Chapter 6 draws on the findings from Chapters 3, 4 and 5 to present an analysis of BSL from all three metafunctional perspectives. As will be seen throughout this work, while it is possible to analyse these metafunctions separately, particularly when attempting to simplify its description, it is nevertheless important to recognize their interaction. Finally, in Chapter 7, the work is drawn to a close as the significance of some core findings is reviewed, and a variety of future pathways for investigation is provided. This is done with the hope that readers of this work will feel sufficiently intrigued and informed to want to build on what is provided here.

Given the themes that have been explored in this chapter and the broader domain of this book, a brief closing note regarding my position as a hearing researcher in a deaf space is required. While I have knowledge of BSL, its sociocultural developments and of deaf communities overall, I nonetheless form part of the surrounding hearing community. Researching a linguistic community when being socioculturally situated outside of that group is nothing novel, as can be seen in multiple ethnographic studies (Selleck, 2017). However, I am also aware that caution is required when exercising a potentially problematic power differential.

This chapter has noted that members of deaf communities have been systematically placed in positions of disadvantage for more than a century (if not much longer). Arguably, most of this disadvantage has been – and often continues to be – enforced by those within the hearing community, sometimes under the guise of a 'saviour that nobody asked for', and other times driven by wilful misunderstanding, ignorance and even overt xenophobia. I am a hearing academic, who is also white, male and who is part of the LGBTQ+ community. As such, I acknowledge the factors of my identity that afford the privileges I have in being able to write this work, alongside those aspects of my identity that resonate with sociocultural and historical struggles of deaf communities.

Regardless, within this specific context, my hearing status acts as the most salient, and potentially problematic, fact.

Research that I have performed with members of various deaf communities has occasionally been met with understandable uncertainty and caution: What does this hearing person want to do with (or to) our language? Will he accurately represent our experiences? Will this person just take without reciprocation? These questions and others are all valid and worthy of further discussion. Space does not allow for a more in-depth response, but I confirm my position as follows.

This work is the culmination of many years of research and interaction with many people in regularly overlapping deaf and linguistic spheres. It builds on the findings presented in my doctoral thesis, which could not have been completed without the support of deaf community members of who taught me BSL, who welcomed me to work alongside the community and who gave me insight into the daily realities of the deaf world. To paraphrase a statement from the World Federation of the Deaf (2014), work regarding deaf communities should be performed actively with deaf communities: 'no research about us without us'. This sentiment permits inclusion, fair representation and accuracy of experience, amongst other things. Just as for my doctoral thesis, this current work also serves the same broad purposes: to provide a novel point of view regarding the description and analysis of BSL through a social semiotic lens; to encourage further work and discussion in this area; and to highlight and legitimize the study, use and recognition of sign languages. It is not, and must never be understood as, an argument for a hearing and/or prescriptivist positioning of 'the way BSL users should sign'.

Contextualizing British Sign Language within a Systemic Functional Framework

Systemic Functional Linguistics (SFL) provides a robust approach to the description and analysis of how meaning is made in social terms or, put another way, social semiosis. With a worldwide network of scholars and practitioners, research in this domain has developed in myriad ways since its inception by Halliday (1961/2002), when it was originally entitled 'scale-and-category grammar' (see Martin, 2016; Taverniers, 2011, for more in-depth treatments of this evolution). In its current form, systemic functionalism has been employed in the description and analysis of various languages (e.g. Caffarel, 2006; Halliday and Matthiessen, 2014; Li, 2007; Martin and Doran, 2015; Martin, Doran and Figueredo, 2020; Martin, Quiroz and Figueredo, 2021; Martin et al., 2021). It has also extended into realms such as education and pedagogy (Halliday, 1991/2007; Rose and Martin, 2012), language acquisition and development (Halliday, 1975; Painter, 1989, 2015), computational approaches (Fawcett, 2008; Matthiessen and Bateman, 1991), multimodality (Kress, 2010; Kress and van Leeuwen, 2006), gesture and paralanguage (Hao and Hood, 2019; Martin and Zappavigna, 2019; Ngo et al., 2021) and the domains of Critical/Positive Discourse Analysis (Bartlett, 2018; Martin, 2004; van Leeuwen, 2008).

Christie (2004) notes that systemic functionalism 'offers quite overtly a social theory and a theory of social action. That is, it involves a theory about the nature of social life, a theory of language as a fundamental semiotic system involved in the shaping of social life, and a theory about the possibilities of social change' (p.21). With language forming a pivotal role in this endeavour, it is unsurprising that SFL has been used to address, amongst other things, typological concerns (i.e. descriptions of language use around the world). Mwinlaaru and Xuan (2016) present a detailed review of this work, in terms of both the origins of this endeavour in the Prague school of linguistics (e.g. Jakobsen, 1966) and the identification of the various languages that have been investigated from systemic functional standpoints, such as English, Spanish, Chinese, Indonesian,

Pitjantjatjara and Gooniyandi (see Appendix 1 of Mwinlaaru and Xuan, 2016 for the full list). Martin and Quiroz (2020, 2021) also explicitly address the potential contribution of SFL to functional language typology. However, a noticeable gap remains when it comes to working towards the goal of a holistic applicability of SFL to semiotic systems – a gap that this work aims to assist in reducing. In short, the application of systemic functional frameworks, thoughts, descriptions and analyses to languages in the visual-spatial modality, such as BSL, is yet to gain any significant ground. In fact, the thesis upon which this book is based (Rudge, 2018) along with a handful of research papers forms the extant of research found in this area at the time of writing (see Johnston, 1996, for applications to Auslan; Wille et al., 2018, for applications to Flemish Sign Language; and Rudge, 2015, 2020, 2021, for applications to BSL).

This chapter begins by introducing SFL in relation to five semiotic dimensions of language, providing insight into the theoretical and descriptive assumptions founding SFL. These serve as the foundation through which BSL is presented as a semiotic system in this work. This includes a closer look at the production of BSL (building on information provided in Chapter 1) in terms of the hands, the body and the space around the signer, and how these are posited to 'fit' into a lexicogrammatical rank scale, with extensions where appropriate to provide a visuo-centric description of the phenomena at hand. Other areas addressed include: discussion of the difficulty of categorizing aspects of BSL expression as lexicogrammatical concerns or factors that operate at the plane of expression; understanding of the concept of a 'clause' in BSL and how this has informed the analyses and descriptions presented in this work; and discussion on drawing distinctions between aspects of gestural communication and components in sign languages.

Five semiotic dimensions

From a systemic functional perspective (drawing on Caffarel, Martin and Matthiessen, 2004), there are five semiotic dimensions that must be understood when considering languages as social semiotic systems. These are: *stratification, metafunction, instantiation* (which are classed as the theoretical dimensions), *rank* and *system* (which are classed as the descriptive dimensions). The theoretical dimensions are assumed to be more or less constant between languages (i.e. all languages share features of stratification, metafunction and instantiation), whereas descriptive dimensions may vary substantially (e.g. the rank scales and systems of English and Chinese differ considerably). These five dimensions will be discussed in turn.

Stratification

SFL interprets human languages as stratified systems of meaning. Stratification concerns the distribution of a semiotic system into various levels or 'strata', and how these strata interact with one another. Systemic functionalism recognizes the planes of linguistic content and linguistic expression (to use terms proposed by Hjelmslev, 1693). However, as Matthiessen, Teruya and Lam (2010) explain, within semiotic systems, 'each plane is stratified into two strata' (p.194), so a fuller perspective sees semiotic systems as being composed of four strata: semantics and lexicogrammar, phonology and phonetics (see Figure 2.1).

Note, too, the superordinate stratum of context shown in Figure 2.1, lying outside of the semiotic system but nonetheless surrounding it. SFL has been strongly influenced by Malinowski and Firth, following tenets such as 'a word without linguistic context is a mere figment and stands for nothing by itself, so in the reality of a spoken living tongue, the utterance has no meaning except in the context of situation' (Malinowski, 1923, p.307), and 'the complete meaning

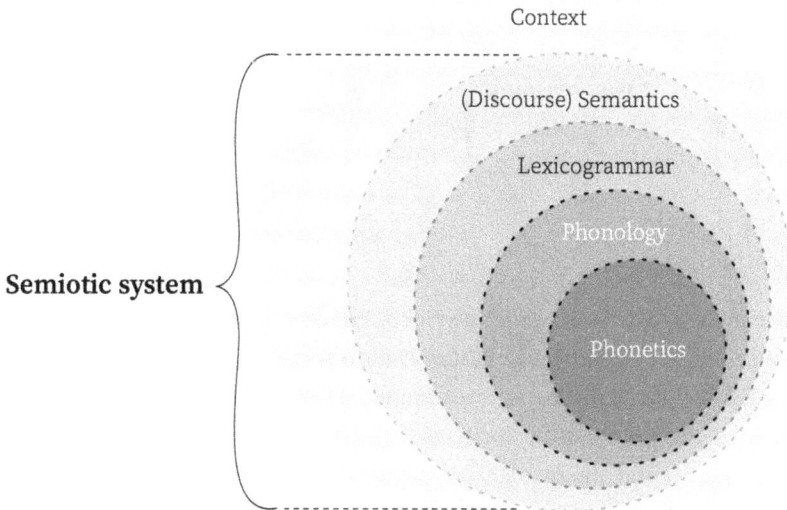

Figure 2.1 A basic schematization of the dimension of stratification.

of a word is always contextual, and no study of meaning apart from a complete context can be taken seriously' (Firth, 1935, p.27). As such, placing a semiotic system within its context is pivotal, and while the definition and delimitation of context are still tricky to fully ascertain, much work has been performed in this regard (see, *inter alia*, Hasan 2014, Leckie-Tarry, 1995, Martin and Rose, 2008; Matthiessen, 2019). Accordingly, descriptions and analyses in later chapters are prefaced with explanations of the communicative contexts in which linguistic production occurred.

Relationships between strata can be understood through the concept of realization: elements at higher strata are realized by elements at lower strata (e.g. lexicogrammar is realized by expression; discourse-semantics is realized by lexicogrammar-realized-by-expression and so on). This wording suggests a unidirectional influence from 'top-down', but the reality is far more complex, as will be elaborated on in the following sections. In short, a dialectic or cogenetic relationship exists between strata, involving the concepts of activation and construal, as highlighted by Hasan (1999):

> If in speaking, the speaker's perception of context *activates* her choice of meanings, then also the meanings meant in speaking *construe* contexts; and the same relation of activation and construal holds, *mutatis mutandis*, between meaning and lexicogrammar.

> (p.223; original emphasis)

This can also be related to the systemic functional concept of resonance across strata: 'The relationship is of a dialectic nature in that contextual values guide linguistic selections, but at the same time they are specified by linguistic selections' (Matthiessen, 2019, pp.23–4).

Metafunction

The second dimension of semiotic systems concerns metafunction: the 'highly generalised functions language has evolved to serve' (Matthiessen, Teruya and Lam, 2010, p.138). In most systemic functional models, three metafunctions are noted – the interpersonal, the ideational (which can be split into the experiential and the logical) and the textual.[1] Of these, the interpersonal (concerned with enacting and negotiation), experiential (concerned with construing experience) and textual (concerned with composition) form the main focus of the present work. The logical metafunction does not prominently feature in this work as it focuses on relationships *between* major units of meaning such as clauses, rather than the relationships that appear *within* them (see Martin, 1988, 1995; Torsello, 1996, for further insight into the place of the logical metafunction in systemic functional analysis).

The metafunctions operate simultaneously within language, such that when linguistic systemic functional analysis is performed, strands of interpersonal, experiential and textual meaning should be discernible. The metafunctions cut across the strata of language, and interact with different aspects of the context of situation. A simplified overview of this is presented in Figure 2.2 showing how, for instance, the interpersonal metafunction is related to the contextual variable of tenor.

Diagrams such as these are useful for understanding the concepts at hand in general terms. It must nonetheless be kept in mind that, like the representation of stratification in Figure 2.1, the reality is more complex than these diagrams can reasonably represent. While three strands of meaning and their associated contextual

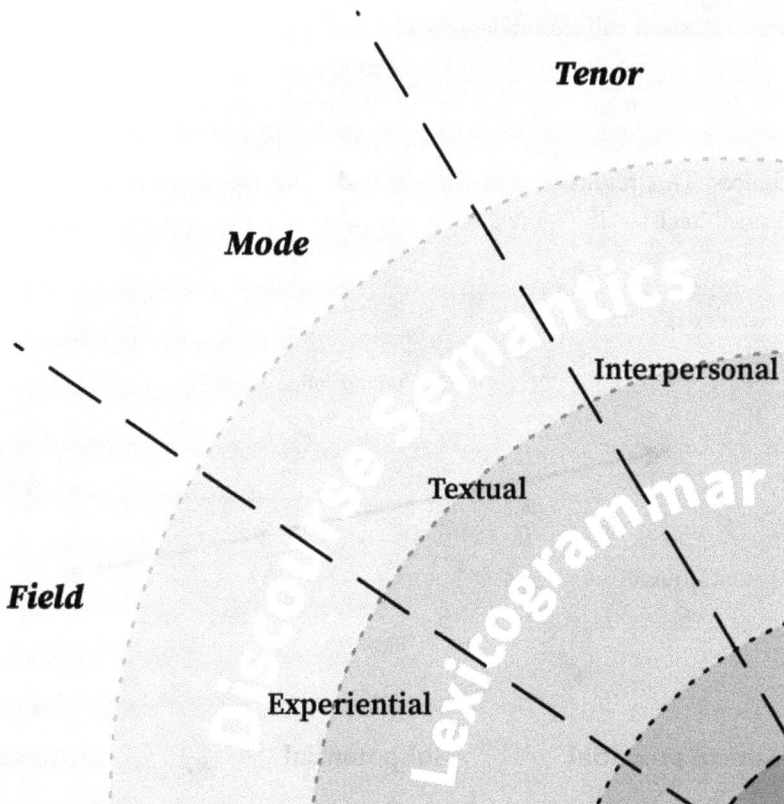

Figure 2.2 A basic schematization of the dimension of metafunction.

variables appear distinct from one other, there is often interaction between them (see Leckie-Tarry, 1995, noting interrelations between field, mode and tenor in terms of predetermination and weighting). This potential for interaction is depicted using broken lines separating the three metafunctional tranches in Figure 2.2.

Instantiation

The final theoretical dimension considers the relationship between individual occurrences (instances) and the generalized sum of all instances. This is schematized in Figure 2.3 (adapting terminology from Matthiessen, 2019; Matthiessen, Teruya and Lam, 2010).

Instantiation can be understood as a cline moving from potential to instance. Contexts of situation are the instances that form the generalized sum of (a) culture. Likewise, texts are the instances that form the generalized sum of (a) language. As suggested earlier, a dialectic relationship is seen between the strata and across the cline (i.e. contexts of situation and texts are cogenetic, as are contexts of culture and language, and so on).

Different choices in language vary in appropriateness in different contexts. Via the incremental application of discourse analysis to a range of texts, observable patterns arise in terms of both contextual variables and linguistic choices. This results in a theoretical mid-point on the cline of instantiation termed 'register' in Figure 2.3. At this point along the cline are the groups of

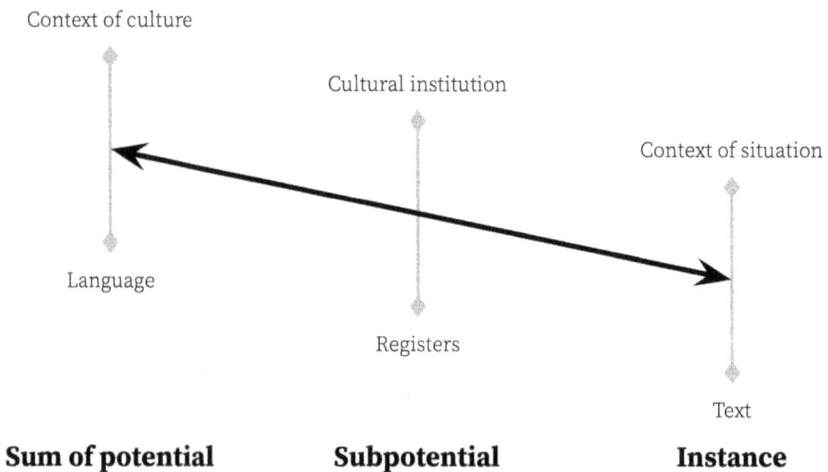

Figure 2.3 A basic schematization of the dimension of instantiation.

features that are commonly selected across strata. For example, the contexts of academic conferences and face-to-face chats with friends relate to distinguishable instances of language usage, but repeated instances of academic conferences or face-to-face chats with friends would reveal common linguistic choices across these individual contexts.

Rank

Rank forms one of the two descriptive dimensions. Rank denotes an organizing principle within a language, most commonly explored at the stratum of lexicogrammar, but also applicable to other strata (e.g. discourse semantics and phonology; see Halliday and Greaves, 2008; Rose, 2007). Rank concerns the composition of, and functional 'points of departure' within, a language.

To take written English as an example, the statement *The foxes had escaped* can be analysed at four ranks: clause (*The foxes had escaped*); group/phrase (*The foxes* as a nominal group and *had escaped* as a verbal group); word (each individual lexeme); and morpheme (the smaller units in words with grammatical functions, e.g. the *-es* plural suffix in *foxes* and the *-d* past tense suffix in *had* and *escaped*). This is elaborated in Table 2.1.

Following Halliday and Matthiessen (2014) and in relation to their principles of constituency in lexicogrammar, there are three fundamentals to bear in mind regarding rank. Firstly, a rank scale must structurally account for each element in a hierarchical and exhaustive fashion, such that higher ranks are made up of one or more elements from the ranks immediately below. As demonstrated in Table 2.1, the clause is composed of two groups, the groups of four words and the words seven morphemes. Secondly, there is potential for rank shift, wherein a unit operating at a higher rank may 'shift' downwards by one rank to operate at that level (e.g. in *The pigeon on the harbour wall*, the prepositional phrase *on the harbour wall* is embedded in a nominal group as the Qualifier). Thirdly, each rank offers 'points of departure' for different functions. This can

Table 2.1 An example of the lexicogrammatical rank scale of English.

clause	The	foxes		had		escaped	
group/phrase	The	foxes		had		escaped	
word	The	foxes		had		escaped	
morpheme	The	fox	-es	ha-	-d	escape	-d

be presented as a function-rank matrix (such as those presented in Halliday and Matthiessen, 2014; Matthiessen, Teruya and Lam, 2010). These identify, for instance, that systems (explained in the following section) in English like TRANSITIVITY and MOOD are found at clause rank, TENSE and QUALIFICATION at group rank, DENOTATION at word rank and so on.

System

The second descriptive dimension is system. Whereas the dimension of rank is concerned with linguistic elements in terms of their composition and order, system is concerned with 'what *could go instead of what*' (Halliday and Matthiessen, 2014, p.22; original emphasis). In other words, both the syntagmatic (i.e. composition and order) and the paradigmatic (i.e. optionality and choice) aspects of language, or 'axes', are included in the systemic functional approach. These axes are inextricably linked within systemic functionalism, such that there is a strong emphasis on axial relations and axial argumentation in linguistic description (see, e.g., Martin, Doran and Figueredo, 2020; Martin, Zhu and Wang, 2013).[2]

A system represents the choices in meaning-making available within any of the abovementioned linguistic strata. System networks are schematized to represent these choices and show, among other things, how systems relate to one another and how meaning is realized though linguistic expression. A simplified example of the English system of interpersonal MOOD is presented in Figure 2.4, identifying core terminology used including system names, entry conditions,

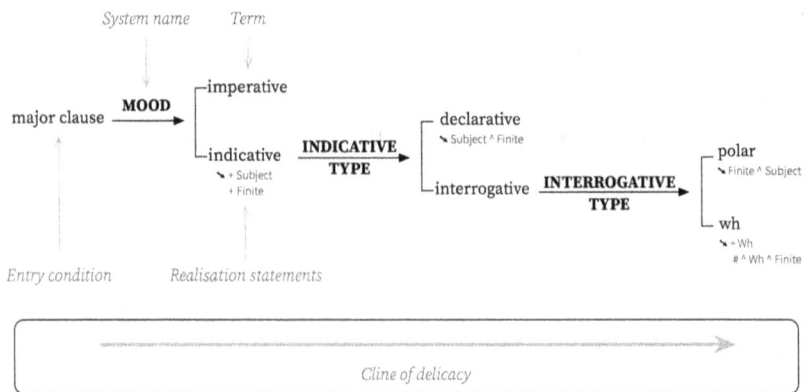

Figure 2.4 A basic schematization of the English MOOD system network.

terms and realization statements. Figure 2.4 also presents the theoretical cline between grammar and lexis as one of delicacy (i.e. grammar as least delicate and lexis as most delicate; hence the use of 'lexicogrammar' in SFL so as not to represent these as two modular phenomena; see Matthiessen, 1995).

System networks are read from left to right: when the entry condition is fulfilled, the system is entered and a choice can be made. This choice, which may not always be a binary one, may then act as a further entry condition into another system, and it may also involve a realization statement (i.e. the grammatical function that is necessary to realize the feature selected). For instance, in the English system of MOOD, the feature [indicative] can be chosen, involving both a realization statement ('add a Subject and Finite to the clause') and entry into the system of INDICATIVE TYPE. If [declarative] were the feature chosen in this latter system, then the realization statement indicates that these functional elements should be syntagmatically ordered as Subject followed by Finite.

Systems and system networks can range in terms of their complexity and capability. The example provided in Figure 2.4 is deliberately simplified for ease of comprehension. Far more complex examples for English can be found in Halliday and Matthiessen (2014), and an explanation of common systemic conventions is available in most literature focused on this subject (e.g. Appendix 2 of Martin, Zhu and Wang, 2013).

Situating BSL within the systemic functional dimensions

As noted above, the five dimensions can be split in terms of their 'theoretical' or 'descriptive' status. Those falling into the former category (i.e. stratification, metafunction and instantiation) are understood to be more typologically stable, while those falling into the latter (i.e. rank and system) are more susceptible to variation depending on the language under scrutiny. So, in comparing languages such as English, Mandarin Chinese and now BSL, we would expect each to find stratified systems that are divisible into a metafunctional tripartite and that offer similar potential in terms of instantiation. Yet, their rank organization and system network structure would be expected to differ, potentially considerably.

This section presents various considerations that arise when attempting to describe BSL in a systemic functional framework. Now that further systemic functional theory has been presented, this section revisits and elaborates on what was presented in the previous chapter.

Revisiting BSL production and its relationship to rank

In Chapter 1, it was noted that BSL has three broad elements of productive expression: the manual (that which is produced with the hands); the non-manual (that which is produced with embodied features such as the eyebrows and mouth) and the spatio-kinetic (that which occurs within the signing space). To fully understand BSL production, it was argued that these three elements are simultaneously observed. However, as examples in Chapter 1 also alluded to, accurate representations of a dynamic, three-dimensional language such as BSL are difficult to fully convey when written down. If no visual representation is available, glossing may be used, although this requires the use of another language's written system or, in more specialized instances, deliberately designed written systems like HamNoSys (Hanke, 2004). In BSL, annotation conventions exist for research purposes thanks to work on the BSL Corpus Project at University College London (Cormier et al., 2017), permitting more accurate and standardized coding using letters and symbols found within written English. Nevertheless, for all its benefits, this system still involves an overall methodological restriction found when using a written language to represent a sign language: the complexity and nuances of the signed production cannot be neatly conveyed (although the same may also be argued for representations of spoken language).

Despite this restriction, it is still possible to perform and report on reasonably deep analyses of BSL. From a systemic functional perspective, we can begin to explore this by considering what a rank scale for the lexicogrammar of BSL may look like, considering that this is one of the descriptive dimensions that is susceptible to variation between languages. A more detailed exploration of this is offered in Rudge (2020), but the following provides an overview of the scale.

A short BSL production is used as an example: CAR PT:DET DC:CAR-PASSES-QUICKLY (broadly translated as 'That car sped past'; see Figure 2.5). CAR is produced as a fully lexical sign with internal movement, PT: represents a pointing sign (in this case, a determiner), and DC: indicates that a depicting construction is used with one hand representing the previously mentioned CAR.[3]

The composition of this production when glossed as CAR PT:DET DC:CAR-PASSES-QUICKLY appears straightforward. The whole unit appears to express the relationship between an entity and an occurrence – a specific car is moving at a certain pace. Within this unit are two sub-units that represent nominal aspects (CAR PT:DET) and verbal aspects (DC:CAR-PASSES-QUICKLY). Within the nominal unit are further separable units: CAR; PT:DET; and so on. Consequently, a compositional breakdown of three levels is observable: a larger

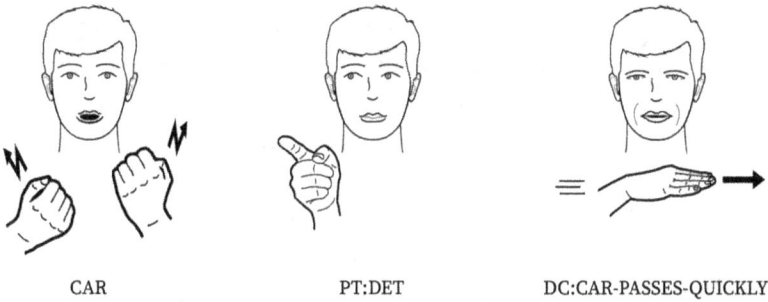

Figure 2.5 CAR PT:DET DC:CAR-PASSES-QUICKLY.

clause-like unit; smaller group-like units; and even smaller units which appear to equate to individual signs.

The English lexicogrammatical rank scale presented in Table 2.1 showed four ranks: clause, group/phrase, word and morpheme. Other languages such as Mandarin Chinese (following Li, 2007) use only three ranks: clause, group and word. Based on the brief analysis of the production in Figure 2.5 so far, an initial assumption could be that BSL has a rank scale like that of Mandarin Chinese. However, an issue soon appears. At this stage, we have analysed a stretch of BSL using a written representation in another language. These representations as they stand do not transcribe the full productive complexity of BSL in terms of its simultaneous usage of manual, non-manual and spatio-kinetic resources. Therefore, if the goal is to represent the lexicogrammatical constituency of language via a rank scale, then these three productive components of the visual-spatial modality need to be considered. This is presented in the rank scale for the lexicogrammar of BSL in Table 2.2.

Table 2.2 An example of the lexicogrammatical rank scale of BSL.

	clause	CAR	PT:DET	DC:CAR-PASSES-QUICKLY
	group/phrase	CAR	PT:DET	DC:CAR-PASSES-QUICKLY
	word	CAR	PT:DET	DC:CAR-PASSES-QUICKLY
morpheme	*Manual*	CAR	PT	RH = CAR classifier
	Non-manual	"car"		Cheeks puffed; furrowed brows; etc.
	Spatio-kinetic		'x'	'x' → in front of signer; fast movement

The proposed rank scale may be interpreted in a similar fashion to what is seen in other rank scales regarding clause, group and word.[4] At morpheme rank, the three aforementioned meaning-bearing elements of BSL production are incorporated, and it is the 'vertical combinations' of these morphemic elements that form the composition of the word rank: CAR is composed of the manual sign and an English mouthing; PT:DET is composed of a manual pointing sign and a location in the signing space (arbitrarily noted here as 'x'); and DC:CAR-PASSES-QUICKLY comprises a greater level of productive complexity, incorporating the signer's right hand (RH) as the classifier handshape for CAR, non-manual elements of the cheeks being puffed out, furrowed brows, and a narrower eye aperture (combining to give an idea of intensity regarding the speed of the vehicle), and a movement passing from location 'x' in front of the signer at pace.

Depending on the productive modality under investigation, a key difference may therefore be highlighted. In the spoken and written modalities, the morphemic composition can be generally split in a linear fashion to a reliable degree (i.e. breaking up parts of the text 'one after another'). In the visual-spatial modality, such as that used by BSL, productive simultaneity means that it is not only a linear concatenation that creates meaning, but also the simultaneous combination of elements at any given moment.

An important point to note regarding Table 2.2 is that the morpheme rank is not in itself displayed in a compositional hierarchy, as is suggested in the ranks of clause, group and word (i.e. 'manual' is neither a rank higher than, nor composed of, 'non-manual' or 'spatio-kinetic'). All three morphemic elements operate in tandem, though this is tricky to show in a two-dimensional table. Regardless, all three need to be present to accurately represent the full compositional nature of BSL. As and when more research progresses in sign languages from SFL perspectives, it may also come to pass that these individual morphemic divisions provide specific 'points of departure' for linguistic functions (i.e. in a function-rank matrix).

Lexicogrammatical or phonological?

The proposed lexicogrammatical rank scale of BSL in Table 2.2 captures the complexities of BSL production at various levels to a good degree. However, there are aspects of the language that still contribute to meaning that are not necessarily found within the lexicogrammatical stratum, and thereby would not appear in this rank scale.

Taking again the example of CAR PT:DET DC:CAR-PASSES-QUICKLY (see Figure 2.5), it is possible for a signer to produce both CAR and PT:DET with raised eyebrows scoping across both manual signs. Unlike the analysis provided in Table 2.2, the change in the position of the eyebrows does not form part of CAR and PT:DET at morpheme rank in the same way that the mouthing of 'car' or the location in signing space does. The use of raised eyebrows is nonetheless meaningful. As will be discussed in Chapter 5, the eyebrows can be associated with the textual metafunction in terms of identifying information structure and prominence.

The eyebrows are argued to be operating here in a phonological manner (i.e. related to intonation) rather than a strictly lexicogrammatical one. This proposed distinction will be returned to at appropriate points throughout the work, but at this stage, it suffices to make two points. Firstly, the relationship between the strata of lexicogrammar and phonology, and their resultant combinations for realizations in the discourse semantic stratum, has been studied and identified in other languages. Halliday and Greaves (2008), for instance, provide a thorough exploration of English phonological systems including TONE, TONALITY and TONICITY, demonstrating that these 'function directly as the realization of systems in the grammar' (p.47) and do so across metafunctions. For example, in interpersonal terms, selections in the phonological system of TONE interact with lexicogrammatical choices, often creating 'incongruent' realizations: saying *He hasn't arrived* (i.e. a [declarative] selection) with a rising intonation results in something more akin to a question (i.e. an [interrogative] selection). Similarly, Quiroz (2018) demonstrates the interaction between interpersonal concerns and phonological systems in basic contrasts in the Chilean Spanish system of MOOD (i.e. intonation as a fundamental distinction between [declarative] and certain [interrogative] types). As such, to find similar phonological effects occurring in BSL is not surprising.

The second point to note is that, despite these typological similarities, there is a potential difficulty when attempting to accurately identify whether elements of production are lexicogrammatical or phonological in their semiotic nature. This is due to the multifunctionality of embodied articulators. As alluded to above, for instance, the eyebrows can realize both lexicogrammatical and phonological aspects, but there is nothing deliberately expressive that categorizes the eyebrows as realizing meaning in one stratum or the other. Instead, it is necessary to observe the element in question in relation to the rest of the expression. This is an issue that has been noted outside of systemic functional perspectives, such as Mapson's (2014, 2020) investigations into politeness marking in BSL through non-manual aspects: 'in BSL, politeness is predominantly conveyed through specific accompanying non-manual features. Difficulties with analysis are compounded by *the multi-functionality of these features, and the simultaneous production of multiple features*' (2014, p.180; emphasis added). Although the current work does not address politeness in the sense that Mapson does, the same analytical difficulties are nonetheless encountered.[5]

Clarifying and identifying the 'clause' in BSL

As found in other systemic functional descriptions of languages noted so far, the typical lexicogrammatical unit under observation is the clause. The clause is a notion that is broadly accepted across language-based disciplines, to the extent that literature dealing with the clause as a unit of analysis rarely seems to define it. Its identification within sign languages such as BSL, though, requires further commentary.

From a systemic functional perspective, the clause is at the highest rank of the lexicogrammatical rank scale, and it is the point that 'unifies different metafunctional strands of meaning' (Matthiessen, Teruya and Lam, 2010, p.72). In descriptions of English, as for various other languages (see, *inter alia*, Caffarel, 2006; Lavid, Arús and Zamorano-Mansilla, 2010; Teruya, 2007), the clause is the point of departure for 'primary' simultaneous lexicogrammatical systems including TRANSITIVITY and MOOD (see Halliday and Matthiessen, 2014). As such, it would be expected that certain core functional elements are identifiable in clauses, permitting accurate comparative analysis. Depending on the metafunctional standpoint being taken, a clause can take on the role of the principal unit of exchange and negotiation (i.e. interpersonally), of representation (i.e. experientially) or of the broader message at play (i.e. textually).

From more formal perspectives, such as those found in popular textbooks on general linguistics, definitions of 'clause' vary. For instance, in Börjars and Burridge's (2010) explanation of English grammar, a clause is defined in terms of its components, with the lexical verb as central: '[a clause] is a linguistic unit which is built around a lexical verb; it contains all the elements required by the verb, and often also some optional modifiers' (p.295). Tallerman's (2015) work on syntax more generally, however, notes that 'some languages [...] allow independent clauses consisting of a subject and a predicate that is non-verbal' (p.79). Not only does this question the centrality of a lexical verb typologically, but Tallerman also notes that this can occur in English clauses: 'We can omit the copula to express disbelief: *Zainal a teacher? Who would ever have believed it?*' (p.52; original emphasis). Despite the grammatical centrality of the clause, 'clause' is neither defined nor addressed as a specific term in some introductory literature (e.g. Yule, 2014). Consequently, relying purely on formal perspectives to understand a clause can lead to confusion.

A combination of functional and structural views is therefore useful in this work, particularly as most of the current work investigating sign languages does so from broadly form-based paradigms. In other words, identifying a clause in terms of its structure, particularly when working in an understudied communicative modality, can assist when trying to investigate the clause in terms of its functional potential. This is visible in previous works that have attempted to delimit clauses in sign languages, such as Hansen and Heßmann's (2007) analysis using manual and non-manual productions in Deutsche Gebärdensprache (DGS; German Sign Language) to identify related topics, predicates, adjuncts and conjuncts. This is also seen in Gabarró-López's (2019) use of the Basic Discourse Unit in both Langue des signes de Belgique francophone (LSFB; French Belgian Sign Language) and Llengua de signes catalana (LSC; Catalan Sign Language).

Closer to BSL, much work has been performed by colleagues working with Auslan regarding clauses and their composition. While earlier work applied systemic functional theory to Auslan (e.g. Johnston, 1996), more contemporary works use approaches such as Role and Reference Grammar (RRG) – a similarly functionalist paradigm with distinct analytical and theoretical motivations (see Butler, 2003, for an in-depth comparison of structural-functional linguistic frameworks). In papers such as Hodge (2013) and Hodge and Johnston (2014), the clause as a unit in a sign language is problematized, indicating that it cannot be completely argued that there are 'constructions that correspond to linguistic definitions of "clause" or if they represent another type of utterance' (Hodge and Johnston, 2014, p.271). The term clause-like unit (CLU) is adopted to represent this interpretation:

> Units smaller than discourse level that constitute a descriptive category of possible candidates for Auslan-specific constructions, and that correspond with various types of communicative moves in face-to-face interaction [but] not 'clause level' in the sense of 'level of analysis where all units are clauses'.

> (ibid.)

A later paper by Johnston (2019) further explores clausehood in Auslan and defines clauses as 'meaningful symbolic utterance units that assert something about the world, and/or are a turn in a communicative interaction' (p.945). Johnston still notes the use of CLU as a term within the context of sign languages, yet presents both methodological insight and analysis of units comparable with clauses in other modalities. He suggests that while the CLU is a notion to bear in mind when observing compositional aspects of a sign language, it should not act as a roadblock to performing such analyses based on theories that have been developed from primarily spoken and written data. In short, between-modality differences exist, but they are not obstructive. As such, the remainder of this work will use 'clause' for equivalent units in BSL, primarily for ease of integration with systemic function theory overall. Where exceptions to this occur (i.e. where something 'clause-like' is present), these will be addressed appropriately.

This leads to the following question: if clauses can be observed in a language operating the visual-spatial modality, what do they look like? As in speech, sign language production may not always present immediately obvious points for defining and delimiting lexicogrammatical units. Just as a written sentence can be spoken aloud without the corresponding whitespace found between each word (e.g. *each and every* pronounced /iːʧənɛvri/), so too can a stretch of BSL have no immediately identifiable points at which one manual sign transitions into another. Nonetheless, through methodical and repeated observations of BSL productions which consider the manual, non-manual and spatio-kinetic elements of production, it is possible to split signed production into clauses.

For the data presented in each of the following chapters, a methodological approach reminiscent of that found in Rudge (2018) and Johnston (2019) was used to move from raw visual data to segmented lexicogrammatical units. The EUDICO Linguistic Annotator (ELAN, 2020) was used in this endeavour, permitting time-aligned annotations of videos across multiple independent tiers (e.g. one tier was used to segment and gloss individual signs, another tier was organized into longer segments and annotated with broad English translations, and so on; see Figure 2.6). Using written tiers not only helps to create a searchable version of the visual data, but it also allows for a visual representation of co-occurring manual, non-manual and spatio-kinetic features found in BSL expression. In a similar fashion to Sandler's (1999) model of the superarticulatory array (which can pinpoint co-occurrences and shifts between different lexicogrammatical units), ELAN proves beneficial in sign language

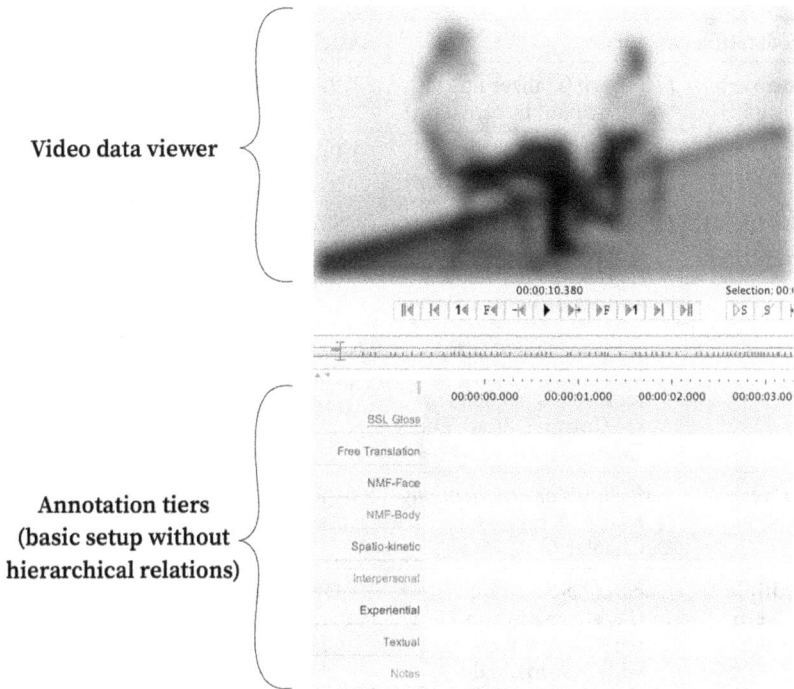

Figure 2.6 A screenshot of the ELAN interface.

clause segmentation as the non-manual and spatio-kinetic dimensions can often assist in finding clause boundaries: '[when] cues are aligned together, they can signal a shift to a new sentence or clause' (Padden, 2015, p.150).

After organizing and annotating tiers, the data were reviewed to identify potential clause candidates. Under the assumption that a clause represents some sort of turn or assertion, core predicating elements (as listed in Table 2.3) were first identified, alongside the elements relating to that predication (i.e. nominal elements such as DOOR, including pointing signs such as PT:PRO1SG) and any other elements that were more peripheral in nature yet nonetheless related to the unit under observation (e.g. temporal or locative adjuncts, and so on). Once broadly delimited, these were compared to associated cues in the non-manual and spatio-kinetic tiers to confirm or further refine the clause boundaries. This was particularly useful in instances where signs were ellipted, where there were dependency relationships between clauses (i.e. hypotactic relationships) and where more complex predicating elements were found. Examples of clauses and

Table 2.3 Predication categories and clause types observed in BSL.

Predicating category		BSL clause example	English gloss
One 'verb sign'	*Plain verb* (realizes no participant information)	PT:PRO1SG <u>EAT</u>	I <u>eat</u>
	Indicating verb (realizes participant information)	PT:PRO3PL <u>PRO3PL -ASK-PRO1SG</u>	They <u>ask</u> me
Enactment	*Depicting construction* (use of a proform/classifier to represent a participant and action)	BUS <u>DC:VEHICLE-REVERSING</u>	The bus <u>reversed</u>
	Constructed action (use of the signer's body to represent a participant; see Cormier, Smith and Zwets, 2013)	DOG <u>CA: PANTING-DOG</u>	The dog <u>panted</u>
No 'verb signs'	*Verb ellipsis or experientially relational clause* (see Chapter 4)	PT:PRO1SG HAPPY	I (<u>am</u>) happy
Multiple 'verb signs'	*Elaborate predication* (i.e. alternation and repetition of verb signs with non-manual changes; see Hodge and Johnston, 2014)	PT:DET <u>ADJUST CHECK ADJUST CHECK</u>	(I) <u>frequently adjusted and checked</u> that

their associated categories of predication can be seen in Table 2.3 (each of which may be applied to data in other BSL datasets).

As noted in other research that observes the structure and function of sign languages, this methodology requires a significant amount of time due to the requirement to perform numerous passes of the data to ensure that it is sufficiently annotated. Although advances in computational and corpus linguistic methods have seen a reduction in the time required to automatically annotate or tag parts of speech in written languages, being able to do the equivalent in any sign language – particularly with data obtained without any automated measurement devices – is still a long way off (see, however, Bragg et al., 2019 for recent insight into where this and similar technological concerns currently reside). The present method thus takes a significant amount of effort to complete, but that in itself may also be viewed as a positive methodological upshot, as it allows for deep consideration of all instances rather than potentially falling into the trap of overreliance on automatic annotation.

Sign language and gesture – A necessary division?

A final point of interest that both impacts the abovementioned methodology and extends to more theoretical debate is necessary to address before closing this chapter. When using a spoken language such as English, particularly in face-to-face contexts, it is not uncommon to observe co-speech gesture and the use of different embodied articulators expressing a kind of communicative function. This has been a point of interest for several decades (see Kendon, 2004 as a core work in this area) with such concerns now starting to gain traction in the systemic functional domain (e.g. Hao and Hood, 2019; Martin and Zappavigna, 2019; Martinec, 2004, 2005; Ngo et al., 2021).

Co-speech gesture, as its name suggests, can be identified because it occurs in tandem with speech – the deictic *that,* for instance, might be uttered alongside a pointing gesture to an object in a room. Or, during the production of *He was really surprised,* the speaker's eyes may widen, alongside a subtle head nod, to affirm the veracity of the statement. Usefully, the split between speech and gesture is marked through the different modalities that are employed: the oral-aural for the former and the visual-spatial for the latter (cf. verbal gesture; Shintel and Nusbaum, 2007). However, assuming that gesture is not restricted to co-occurrence with speech, questions then arise when considering gesture and sign languages as they both operate in the visual-spatial modality. For instance, where does a gesture 'end' and a sign 'begin?' If this division is not clear, when analysing and describing a sign language such as BSL, how can we be sure that we are not blurring the lines between that which is 'sign' and that which is not? Conversely – and more critically given the inherently multimodal nature of human communication overall – should we just embrace this blurring? These questions implicate both linguistic and sociocultural concerns and will be briefly addressed here.

From linguistic perspectives, the study of gesture has helped to shed light on numerous aspects including language evolution (Everett, 2017), the mechanisms of the human brain (Dick et al., 2012) and, more recently, the relationships between and typologies of gesture and grammar (Harrison, 2018). In terms of linguistic description, the visual and multimodal turn is now in full swing, with scholars such as Perniss, Özyürek and Morgan (2015), to name a few, noting that 'our human language capacity is multimodal in nature and conveys information at different semiotic and representational levels' (p.8). It is also stated that gestures are multifunctional in their nature and that 'a "pigeonhole" view on gestural functionality does not do justice to the multifarious nature of gesture use in natural discourse' (Kok et al., 2016, p.38). In their extensive consideration of the split between gesture and sign, Goldin-Meadow and Brentari (2017) further state that 'gesture is central to language and is not merely an add-on [and] a full treatment of language needs to include both the more categorical (sign or speech) and the more imagistic (gestural) components regardless of modality' (p.2).

In accepting that gesture forms part of the communicative picture and is not auxiliary to the point of its dismissal, it would therefore be understandable to try to incorporate gestural elements into a linguistic description of a sign language, and to even ask whether the division of 'sign' and 'gesture' is a necessary one in descriptive works. Indeed, Goldin-Meadow and Brentari (2017) identify that such a distinction has offered numerous linguistic, neurological and psychological insights, but that there are also 'descriptive phenomena that do not require a categorical division between gesture and sign' (p.14). From a sociocultural perspective, and resonating with discussions in Chapter 1, it must be remembered that even as recently as a few decades ago, languages like BSL were not viewed as fully fledged semiotic systems, but rather as a 'pantomime or a *language of gestures*' (p.1; emphasis added). A pitfall thereby appears that, if not navigated successfully, could easily threaten the progress made regarding the status and recognition of sign languages. The 'recombination' of BSL with gesture may lead to a hasty conclusion that BSL is pantomimic in nature, rather than linguistic.

It is hoped that this is not the conclusion that the reader will draw from this work, given that the approach taken here is not one of relegation. This work does take a holistic perspective in the communications that are analysed, instead of attempting to find a gesture-sign split. However, this is performed in the spirit of (systemic) functional frameworks and descriptive techniques. Namely, that it is more advantageous to view each component of a production and their sum in order to understand the semiotic labour being exerted, rather than setting considerably blurred boundaries and potentially eliminating essential data from the process. This is neatly summarized by Kusters and Sahasrabudhe (2018):

> The distinction between gesturing and signing is fluid, changeable, negotiable and context-dependent [...]. This means that, what one person sees as signing, the other may regard as gesturing [...] and what people mean by these labels may vary.
>
> (p.62)

This likewise resonates with Kusters et al.'s (2017) exploration of the semiotic repertoire, wherein communication is understood without a 'strict distinction between named languages, and [...] no distinction between linguistic and non-linguistic' (p.223). The semiotic repertoire 'departs from the idea that languages are bounded systems' (p.228), allowing for flexibility and exhaustiveness in descriptions that may have previously been restricted by overarching categorizations.

In summary, rather than attributing parts of communication to 'sign' and others to 'gesture', the whole communication can be viewed as a complete system with semiotic potential.[6] Again, the intention is not to relegate BSL to a system of pantomime. This perspective instead moves with our ever-broadening understandings of the multimodal complexity of human communication, querying that which is deemed linguistic, and accepting that it is likely more complicated than was once assumed.

Summary

SFL offers a robust framework in which social semiosis can be effectively described and interrogated. The purpose of this chapter was to demonstrate, at an introductory level, that despite the lack of full descriptions of sign languages from systemic functional perspectives, it is nevertheless possible to take core theoretical and descriptive dimensions of SFL – stratification, metafunction, instantiation, rank and system – and apply them to a language operating in the visual-spatial modality. Doing so provides support to the adaptable nature of systemic functional frameworks while also offering a basis from which future work can grow, whether focusing on BSL, another sign language or embodied communication more generally.

The second half of this chapter offered some further points for consideration prior to moving into the core elements of this work, including several methodological factors employed in BSL analysis. Discussing these points here ensures that later chapters can be understood with greater insight, and provides further points of interrogation both within the systemic functional domain and beyond: How might a modified rank scale impact current and future descriptions of semiotic systems? What aspects of BSL (if any) can we securely attribute to the lexicogrammatical or phonological strata? To what extent does the concept of a clause apply to a language such as BSL? How far should we

concern ourselves with the gesture-sign distinction in descriptive works such
as this? These questions may be argued for some time, but their consideration
alone is sufficient at this stage of combining SFL with BSL.

With the above in mind, it is now possible to further explore and describe
BSL in systemic functional terms. I begin with the interpersonal metafunction
(Chapter 3), followed by the experiential metafunction (Chapter 4) and finally
the textual metafunction (Chapter 5). Each metafunction is explored in turn and
to greater depth than that which was presented in the current chapter. It was also
noted in this chapter that these metafunctions operate simultaneously, and so
Chapter 6 draws on all three metafunctions, presenting an analysis of BSL that
considers three perspectives on the same stretch of discourse.

Throughout Chapters 3, 4 and 5, attention will also be paid to the creation of
system networks, resulting in a culminative 'grand network' in Chapter 6. While
this network might be seen as comparatively rudimentary when compared to
those seen in works such as Halliday and Matthiessen (2014), it will nonetheless
serve as a stable resource that can be used to explore further data in BSL.

Exploring the Interpersonal Metafunction

From a systemic functional perspective, meaning making is a process linked to the interactions held between communicative participants across contexts. Put another way, language is an act of social semiosis, and for such semiosis to be successful, cooperation between those in communicative situations is required. 'Cooperation', such as it is intended here, goes beyond generic notions such as agreeing with one another to avoid an argument. Rather, cooperation is used in the sense of active and ongoing negotiations between parties in communicative exchanges, allowing phenomena such as requests, demands and presentations of information (and any resultant responses) in a context. This cooperation in exchanges of meaning also permits us to present nuanced stances in relation to aspects that are communicated (e.g. the validity of propositions) or in relation to the person or people we are speaking to or speaking about (e.g. indicating social proximity or distance). Overall, these social, cooperative and negotiable aspects are ascribed the domain of the interpersonal metafunction, and form the focus of this chapter.

To begin, this chapter expands on the interpersonal metafunction in greater depth than was seen in Chapter 2, particularly with regard to how it is understood from the contextual, discourse semantic and lexicogrammatical strata (i.e. from an axial perspective; see Martin, Doran and Figueredo, 2020; Martin, Quiroz and Figueredo, 2021). As the main goal of this book is to provide a preliminary systemic functional description of BSL in lexicogrammatical terms, the chapter will then move into a deeper lexicogrammatical analysis of excerpts from BSL interactions, focusing on the interpersonal perspective to identify and elaborate on the resources that are called on when dealing with this 'interactive' side of language. This analysis will accompany the creation of the foundational interpersonal system networks of MOOD, POLARITY, MODALITY and SOCIAL PROXIMITY. These systems will then combine to form a larger, simultaneous interpersonal system network, which will be illustrated with a short discourse analysis to conclude the chapter.

Incorporating interaction in language

Language, when viewed through an interpersonal lens, is a resource that enables us to communicate, to interact and to establish (or, in some instances, conclude) relationships with others. Through interpersonal resources, we can state, request or demand, we can respond to these communicative actions, and we can express attitudes and evaluations of others, of objects and of phenomena.

To revisit a point noted in Chapter 2, the theoretical dimensions of stratification and metafunction are closely connected: that which is found at the discourse semantic stratum resonates with elements found in context and in lower linguistic strata (e.g. lexicogrammar and phonology); and there are specific elements at each stratum that tend to associate more closely to one of the three metafunctions. So, for example, when interrogating the interpersonal metafunction at the discourse semantic stratum, we are also implicating the inclusion of aspects from 'above', from 'roundabout' and from 'below', or, put more succinctly, from an axial perspective (Martin, Doran and Figueredo, 2020). The focus of this chapter, and of chapters that follow, is predominantly 'from below' (i.e. lexicogrammatical). To provide theoretical background and to assist in framing forthcoming observations, axial perspectives in interpersonal terms are briefly presented and explored.

From above, the interpersonal metafunction relates to the contextual parameter of tenor. This parameter concerns, amongst other things, the roles and relative power held by communicative participants, their familiarity with one another, the assumed formality of the communicative situation and the participants' emotional commitment to the topics under discussion (see, *inter alia*, Eggins, 2004; Hasan, 2014; Leckie-Tarry, 1995). While such aspects are tricky to measure objectively, these are nonetheless salient features within communicative environments: we can reliably comment on and compare the formality of a job interview with the informality of dinner with friends, the differences in identity and expression when switching between the role of a student in the morning and the role of a caregiver in the evening, and so on. Combined, these different contextual variables will influence, and be influenced by, the choices that we make in linguistic production.

From roundabout, several discourse semantic systems operate simultaneously with regard to the interpersonal metafunction.[1] This includes SPEECH FUNCTION: a system incorporating options during the negotiation of discourse in terms of what is being communicated and in which direction this communication

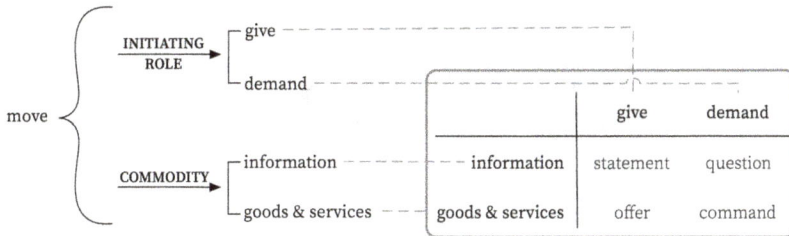

Figure 3.1 A basic schematization of the system of SPEECH FUNCTION.

occurs. More specifically, SPEECH FUNCTION presents insight into the move structures in dialogic interaction, wherein we find a distinction with regard to the commodity 'under negotiation' (e.g. information or goods/services) and whether this is being provided by, or is desired by, the communicative partner. Figure 3.1 presents a simplified version of SPEECH FUNCTION based on Halliday and Matthiessen (2014), demonstrating how simultaneous sub-systems can result in four broad choices of initiating moves in dialogue.

The four resulting combinations shown in Figure 3.1 give an idea of how the notion of 'interpersonal' can be understood in the current context: each option provides a basis to which an interactive partner can respond in a negotiated dialogue based on goals, desires and relational aspects (e.g. aspect of tenor, such as power and solidarity). However, there are numerous levels of complexity not demonstrated here. For instance, while there appear to be four initiating options, the realization of these options from below (i.e. lexicogrammatically) is not strictly one-to-one, as will be elaborated in the following section. Furthermore, an interactive dialogue understandably consists of more than just an initiating move. In Halliday and Matthiessen (2014), initiating moves may also be paired with responses falling into the binary categories of 'expected' and 'discretionary', such that an offer, for instance, may be accepted or rejected respectively. Berry (1981), Ventola (1987) and later Martin and Rose (2007) and Martin (2018) expand on these complexities further and move into more complex exchange structures and the related system of NEGOTIATION found in the discourse semantic stratum, which 'allows for exchanges consisting of between 1 and 5 moves, in addition to tracking and challenging options' (Martin, 2018, p.8).

The main lexicogrammatical systems of interest here relate predominantly with SPEECH FUNCTION due to this system's 'core' position within communication, as noted by Quiroz (2018):

The conceptualisation of basic speech functions at discourse semantics is generally assumed as valid for human language overall, since speakers engage in comparable negotiation of roles and semiotic commodities across languages. Therefore, all languages are expected to grammaticalise primary speech functions as basic clause mood types specifically associated with them.

(p.143)

Towards an interpersonal grammar of BSL

This section presents the first core contribution of this book: an interpersonal grammar of BSL via the elaboration and exemplification of fundamental lexicogrammatical systems. The system of MOOD, which is most closely associated with the realization of choices in SPEECH FUNCTION found at the discourse semantic stratum (as discussed above), is explored alongside arguments for the core interpersonal functional components of a BSL clause, with a particular emphasis on the Predicator. Furthermore, there will be acknowledgement of how realizations of certain choices in MOOD require elements from the lexicogrammatical stratum besides interactions with the phonological and phonetic strata.

Following the exploration of MOOD are further systems aligning within this metafunction, including POLARITY and MODALITY, which both involve realizations that call on manual and/or non-manual productions in nuanced manners. A further system is also introduced: SOCIAL PROXIMITY. This system relies heavily on the spatio-kinetic elements of BSL and is presented here in a preliminary manner. This is because these spatio-kinetic realizations require further deliberation, but their inclusion is intentional to act as a springboard for future studies.[2]

The data presented here are from numerous dyadic interactions recorded between BSL users. In each case, those in communication knew each other to a reasonable extent, having previously communicated with one another on at least two or three occasions prior. Topics of conversation during these recordings were not controlled and it was anticipated that topics would change as the dialogue developed. However, themes such as recounting past experiences, day-to-day activities and future aspirations were common.

The BSL users recorded in this dataset formed part of a larger study in which they were invited to take part in recordings in a semi-controlled setting (i.e. a quiet corner of a public space). This was performed to obtain data that was as naturalistic as possible, although the observational paradoxes of such an endeavour (Labov, 1972) remain applicable.

MOOD

A fundamental move sequence between conversational participants is question and answer: a request is made and a response is put forward. An example of this is provided between signers J and M in Excerpt 3.1a:[3]

[3.1a]

J	BSL	-s-u-e-	PT:POSS3SG	NEW	JOB	WHERE
	English	*Where is Sue's new job?*				

M	BSL	PT:PRO3SG	NOW	BATH	PT:LOC
	English	*She (is) now in Bath.*			

Excerpt 3.1a broadly demonstrates J's information request to M and how M presents the information to J (or, to use the terminology found in SPEECH FUNCTION, J demands information and M gives information). While at first glance this excerpt appears to present a functional distinction in BSL production, Excerpt 3.1a is in fact not sufficiently developed to demonstrate the communicative reality of this interaction. As noted in Chapters 1 and 2, BSL production incorporates more than what is produced on the hands, and it is critical that this information is included in such descriptions and analyses.

Excerpt 3.1b, therefore, elaborates on this two-move sequence by presenting non-manual productive information, with the extent of its co-occurrence with manual signs indicated by an underline. These will be present in excerpts from this point forward, but in trying to balance the productive complexity of BSL with the desire to offer as clear an exemplification as possible, only non-manual elements that are core to the production in question will be presented.

[3.1b]

J	**Non-manual**					brow furrow
	Manual	-S-U-E-	PT:POSS3SG	NEW	JOB	WHERE
		Where (is) Sue's new job?				

M	Non-manual			head nod	
	Manual	PT:PRO3SG	NOW	BATH	PT:LOC
		She (is) now in Bath.			

Excerpt 3.1b provides greater insight into the exchange as relevant non-manual components are now presented: J's eyebrow furrow and M's head nod. Note, too, that these non-manual components can sometimes align with one manual sign (e.g. WHERE) or scope across two or more signs (e.g. BATH PT:LOC).

Taking a few more examples of question-response pairs with this additional non-manual tier, more precise distinctions can be made. The data in Excerpt 3.2 follows a similar move sequence to that of Excerpt 3.1b:

[3.2]

J	Non-manual			brow furrow
	Manual	PT:PRO3SG	START	WHEN
		When (did) she start?		

M	**Manual**	START	LAST-WEEK
		(She) started last week.	

Excerpt 3.2 shows a move sequence like that of Excerpt 3.1b, wherein J again requests information that M provides. Parallels between these include the use of a manual sign to represent the desired information (i.e. WHERE to identify a spatial location; WHEN to identify a temporal location) which are both co-articulated with furrowed eyebrows and syntagmatically positioned at the end of the clause. M's responses, however, differ slightly. In Excerpt 3.1b, several signs were produced with a head nod to provide the information J requested, as well as referring to the person in question via the pronominal pointing sign PT:PRO3SG and the temporal marker NOW. In Excerpt 3.2, M produces the verb sign START and the temporal information requested by J, neither with overt non-manual elements nor with manual repetition of the referent in question (a perspective that will be explored in Chapter 5 – the ellipsis of signs when information is contextually salient or easily recoverable). Nonetheless, this is just as valid a response as what was produced in Excerpt 3.1b, reflecting a pattern seen across this and other datasets used in this work and beyond: a valid move in BSL dialogue does not always require the overt repetition of certain

elements that, in languages such as English, are deemed interpersonally crucial (e.g. the Subject).

Another kind of a question-response sequence, this time by a different pair of signers, is demonstrated in Excerpt 3.3:

[3.3]

S	**Non-manual**			brow raise
	Manual	SUNDAY	SHOP	CLOSE

(Was) the shop closed on Sunday?

L	**Non-manual**	head nod
	Manual	CLOSE

(It was) closed.

Rather than S requesting information that was unknown, as seen in Excerpts 3.1b and 3.2, S instead requests confirmation of an event that L knows (i.e. that the shop in question was closed on Sunday). From a SPEECH FUNCTION perspective, the initiating move in Excerpt 3.3 still fulfils the role of demanding information but does so in a different way: manually, there is no sign produced that identifies or requests a specific type of information, such as WHERE or WHEN; and

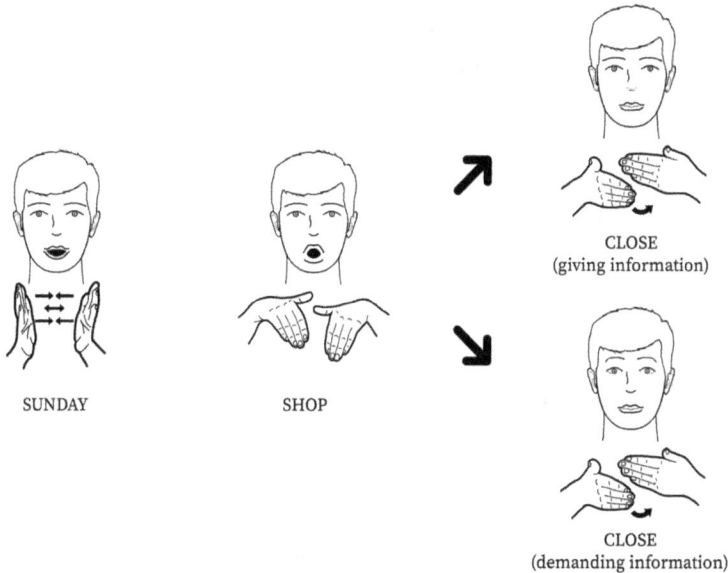

Figure 3.2 An example of non-manual distinctions between moves giving and demanding information.

non-manually, the eyebrows are raised instead of furrowed. L's response bears similarity with that of M in Excerpt 3.2: the response is short, to the point that it is just the repetition and confirmation of the aspect requiring clarification; yet, it is still a valid move in the dialogue. L may have also repeated S's manual signs verbatim, with only differences in eyebrow position distinguishing between giving or demanding information (see Figure 3.2).

Excerpts 3.1b, 3.2 and 3.3 provide insight into three different permissible move types and their realizations in BSL: questions regarding unknown information; questions regarding clarification and statements/presentations of information. In comparison with the low-delicacy interpersonal MOOD systems found in other languages, there appears to be similarity in the kinds of move that can be made at a clause level in BSL: two types of [interrogative] and a [declarative]. These are shown in a basic system network in Figure 3.3. The realizations of these three options require additional explanation.

It is only in requests for unknown information (i.e. [interrogative: elemental]) that the manual component plays a distinguishing part in MOOD, namely, through the use of signs, including WHERE, WHEN, HOW, WHO and so on, to clarify the type of information being requested. Otherwise, these distinctions are made through non-manual components, primarily via the eyebrows.[4] From the excerpts above, it would therefore be tempting to ascribe the eyebrows and their relative height to the lexicogrammatical stratum as they appear to be adding to specific lexicogrammatical aspects of BSL. However, Excerpts 3.4 and 3.5 put this ascription into question:

[3.4]

J	**Non-manual**	brow furrow			
	Manual	PT:PRO3SG	GO	WITH	WHO
		Who (did) he go with?			

[3.5]

L	**Non-manual**	brow raise		
	Manual	COURSE	FINISH	PT:PRO2SG
		(Did) you finish the course?		

Excerpts 3.4 and 3.5 demonstrate how non-manual components can 'scope' across various manual signs in a clause.[5] The eyebrows, when analysed in this way, are argued to be prosodic in nature (i.e. operating at the phonological

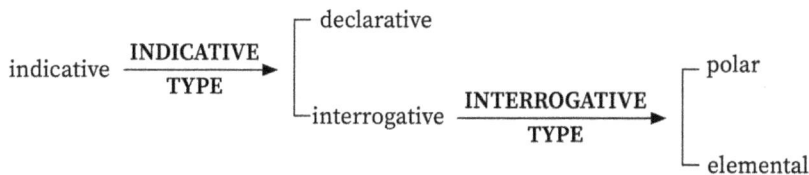

Figure 3.3 A basic schematization of MOOD at low delicacy.

stratum rather than the lexicogrammatical stratum; cf. the use of eyebrows in the lexicogrammatical rank scale in Table 2.2). Works such as Dachkovsky, Healy and Sandler (2013) refer to this as visual intonation or visual prosody, wherein the (typically) non-manual components of a sign language that co-articulate with manual components realize suprasegmental aspects including rhythm, tone and stress. This is somewhat analogous to prosodic systems found in spoken languages, although differences include the modalities of realization and the simultaneous productive potential found in sign languages:

> Unlike the vocal cords in spoken language, which can only vibrate at one frequency at a time, the facial articulations of sign language […] are independent of one another, and can be activated individually or together, to create 'tunes' whose 'tones' occur simultaneously rather than sequentially.
>
> (p.215)

In spite of the extended scoping of the eyebrow positions, from a MOOD perspective, the functions of the clauses in Excerpts 3.4 and 3.5 remain the same as what was observed in previous excerpts.[6] The paradigmatic distinction between [interrogative: elemental], [interrogative: polar] and [declarative], therefore, is realized by manual realizations of interpersonal elements within the clause (at the lexicogrammatical stratum) and the position of the eyebrows (at the phonological stratum) that *co-occur* with these interpersonal elements: raised for [interrogative: polar]; furrowed for [interrogative: elemental] and 'neutral' for [declarative]. Despite being produced in a different communicative modality, this appears to relate closely to the patterns seen in Chilean Spanish (Quiroz, 2018) wherein certain combinations of lexicogrammatical content and phonological tone result in the realization of different choices in MOOD.

In all three of the MOOD choices derived so far, it is argued that the Predicator is the mandatory functional component that needs to be realized to enact these moves. In addition, only for [interrogative: elemental] does an additional function need to appear – the Inquirer – realized lexicogrammatically by signs such as WHERE (requesting locative information), WHO (requesting participant information), HOW (requesting information on the manner of an action) and so on.

The attribution of these functional components can now be presented in excerpts. For the purposes of clarity, the previous four excerpts are repeated below in Excerpts 3.2b to 3.5b with an accompanying tier of interpersonal functions:

[3.2b]

J	Non-manual			brow furrow
	Manual	PT:PRO3SG	START	WHEN
	Interpersonal		Predicator	Inquirer

When (did) she start?

M	Manual	START	LAST-WEEK
	Interpersonal	Predicator	

(She started) last week.

[3.3b]

S	Non-manual			brow raise
	Manual	SUNDAY	SHOP	CLOSE
	Interpersonal			Predicator

(Was) the shop closed on Sunday?

L	Non-manual	head nod
	Manual	CLOSE
	Interpersonal	Predicator

(It was) closed.

[3.4b]

J	Non-manual		brow furrow		
	Manual	PT:PRO3SG	GO	WITH	WHO
	Interpersonal		Predicator		Inquirer

Who (did) he go with?

[3.5b]

L	Non-manual		brow raise	
	Manual	COURSE	FINISH	PT:PRO2SG
	Interpersonal		Predicator	
		(Did) you finish the course?		

To reiterate, the Predicator function is a core functional element in interpersonal systems such as MOOD. As noted previously, as in languages such as Chilean Spanish (Quiroz, 2018), the Predicator permits interaction (i.e. full moves in dialogue) to occur. Excerpts 3.2b–3.5b suggest that this function is realized by a manual sign that is part of the verbal group (i.e. START, CLOSE, GO and FINISH as 'verb signs'), which is again seen in other languages such as Japanese (see Matthiessen, Teruya and Lam, 2010). However, there is an exception to this latter point, demonstrated in Excerpt 3.6:

[3.6]

L	Non-manual		brow raise
	Manual	PT:PRO3SG	HEARING
	Interpersonal		Predicator
		(Is) she a hearing person?	

S	Non-manual	head nod
	Manual	HEARING
	Interpersonal	Predicator
		(She is) a hearing person.

L's question in Excerpt 3.6 ([interrogative: polar] evidenced by the use of raised eyebrows) attributes an audiological status to an individual. S confirms this by repeating the attributed element – HEARING – with a head nod. In both instances, the signs used identify nominal aspects, in this case, PT:PRO3SG referring to a known person and HEARING indicating a description or Epithet (or, in more formal terms, something adjectival). As such, in Excerpt 3.6 and across numerous other clauses seen in everyday BSL interactions, an overt verb sign is not, and does not need to be, expressed. This will be discussed in more detail in Chapter 4, but it suffices here to note that clauses attributing one element to another do so through syntagmatic composition and non-manual features. Put another way, BSL is understood a 'zero copula' language, and no verbal group needs to be realized in these instances.

Nonetheless, the clauses in Excerpt 3.6 still demonstrate valid moves in BSL, and based on prior argumentation, this means that the Predicator function must still be realized despite the lack of a verbal group. It is in these cases the Predicator can be seen to occur in the element that is most interpersonally 'at risk'. Like in previous excerpts, there is an element in L's clause that can be repeated, confirmed, refuted (and so on) in the moves that follow. In this case, this is realized as HEARING.

Before moving on to other systems within the interpersonal metafunction, one final choice of MOOD realization requires attention. This concerns [imperative] choices, relating to 'command' in SPEECH FUNCTION (see Figure 3.1). An example of this is presented in Excerpt 3.7:

[3.7]

M	**Non-manual**		brow furrow; cheek puff
	Manual	PT:PRO3SG	ANGRY
	Interpersonal		Predicator
		He (was) very angry.	

M	**Non-manual**	strong force	
	Spatio-kinetic		
	Manual	CD:[TELL PT:PRO1SG]	
	Interpersonal	Predicator	
		'Tell me!'	

Excerpt 3.7 shows a portion of M's dialogue split into two clauses, the first describing the emotions of a previously identified person and the second reporting what that person signed. As such, the first [declarative] clause is realized in a similar fashion to L's use of two nominal elements in Excerpt 3.6. M indicates that the person being referred to felt angry, the extent of which is communicated using various non-manual features. In the second clause, M uses constructed dialogue (CD; see Cormier, Smith and Zwets, 2013) wherein the direction of M's eye gaze shifts away from the other signer, identifying that M was signing under the 'guise' of another person – in this case, the person referred to in the first clause. This second clause is articulated with a 'strong force' on the non-manual and spatio-kinetic tiers, which realizes the paradigmatic distinction in MOOD between [imperative] and [declarative] choices.

As with [interrogative] choices, visual prosody is implicated in an [imperative] selection in MOOD, albeit with added levels of complexity. The notion of 'force' as noted in Excerpt 3.7 intends to encompass the variety and intensity of non-manual and spatio-kinetic elements that can be used alongside manual signs, including, but not limited to, changes to the speed of production including internal and path movements; more abrupt starts and ends to movements; body leans; variations in eye aperture; and changes in eyebrow position. Furthermore, the nature of the visual-spatial modality is such that each of these productive

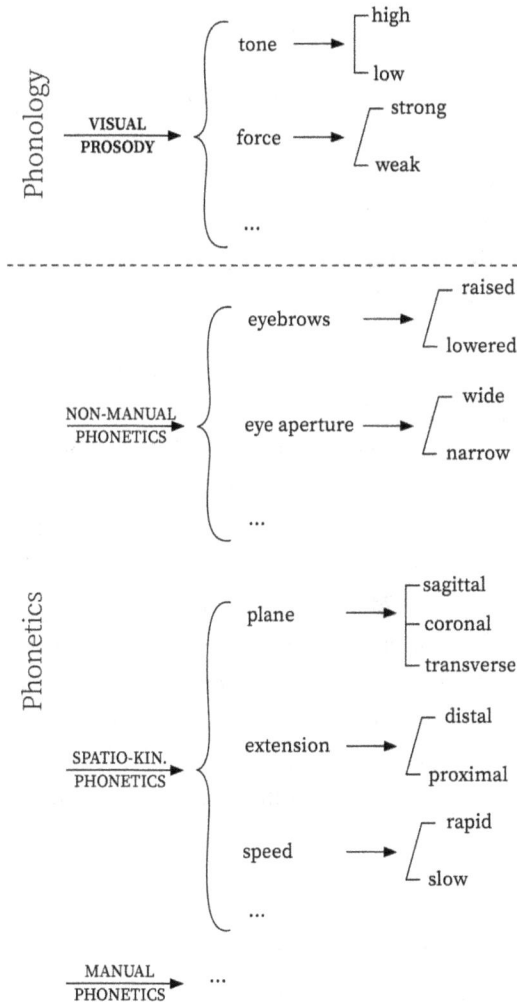

Figure 3.4 Potential system networks at phonological and phonetic strata, including a base system for VISUAL PROSODY.

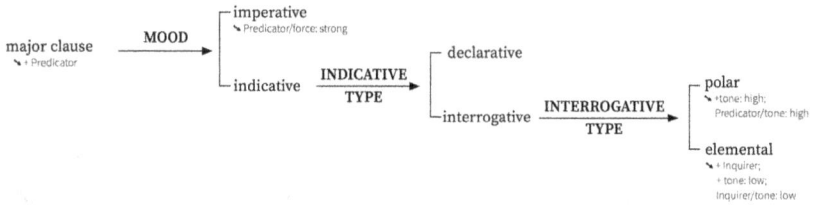

Figure 3.5 BSL system of MOOD.[7]

elements is not discrete in the values that can be expressed. For instance, it is possible to have gradients in the speed of production, multiple angles of body lean, various degrees of eye aperture and so on.

Given that the realm of visual prosody appears to be quite strongly implicated in choices of MOOD, there is a need to recognize the plane of expression further. Although likely to grow in complexity and functionality in future work, Figure 3.4 demonstrates a selection of potential system networks at the phonological and phonetic strata, wherein choices in force in the suggested system of VISUAL PROSODY link to choices available in the phonetic stratum. The non-discrete nature of these choices in expression is represented by the tilted square brackets (e.g. eyebrows can select *between* values of [raised] and [lowered]), and it is a variety of combinations at this phonetic stratum that can result in realizations between [strong] and [weak] force at the phonological stratum. Given the intricacies in realization suggested by Figure 3.4, it is predicted that further types of [imperative] will be identifiable in BSL, eventually leading to a system of IMPERATIVE TYPE. At the time of writing this work, however, studies on imperative structures and functions in BSL and in other sign languages remain under-studied (see Chapter 7 for a summary of next steps in this area of research).

A summary of the system of MOOD for BSL is schematized in Figure 3.5. While elements at the lexicogrammatical stratum play a part in the realizations of these interpersonal paradigmatic choices, strata below also bear significant semiotic weight: for [imperative] and [interrogative] realizations, selections at the phonological stratum need to occur for the distinctions to be realized satisfactorily.

POLARITY

We now move on to address some of the other lexicogrammatical systems that are aligned with the interpersonal metafunction, beginning with POLARITY. This system concerns 'the resource for assessing the arguability value of a clause'

(Matthiessen, Teruya and Lam, 2010, p.161) or, more simply, that which permits a language user to express things such as 'yes' (positive) and 'no' (negative).

As alluded to in the above exploration of MOOD, the Predicator function and non-manual elements of BSL both play a part in this system. This is visible in two simple question-response pairs shown in Excerpts 3.8 and 3.9:

[3.8]

B	Non-manual			<u>brow raise</u>
	Manual	NEW	CAR	BLACK
	Interpersonal			Predicator
		(Is) the new car black?		

A	Non-manual	<u>headshake</u>
	Manual	BLACK
	Interpersonal	Predicator
		(It is) not black.

[3.9]

S	Non-manual			<u>brow raise</u>
	Manual	-p-e-t-e-r-	PT:PRO3SG	TEXT$_{2SG}$
	Interpersonal			Predicator
		Did Peter text you?		

L	Non-manual	<u>headshake</u>	
	Manual	TEXT$_{1SG}$	PT:PRO3SG
	Interpersonal	Predicator	
		He didn't text me.	

In Excerpt 3.8, B's request for confirmation on the colour of the car in question is met with A's response that indicates [negative] polarity, realized using a headshake co-occurring with the repetition of the Predicator. This same co-occurrence is observed in L's response to S's question in Excerpt 3.9, although L's headshake scopes across both the Predicator and the pointing sign PT:PRO3SG (note, too, that this neither 'negates the referent' identified by the pointing sign, nor creates a 'double negative' conundrum as is often seen in English sentences). If A's and L's headshakes were replaced with head nods – or without any such head movement – then the responses would have realized a [positive] polarity and, in these instances, confirmation of B's and

S's statements rather than their refutation. A selection of [positive] polarity is exemplified in Excerpt 3.10, wherein J first confirms a question posed by M with a head nod, and then adds further information without any marked non-manual production:

[3.10]

M	Non-manual			brow raise	
	Manual	PARTY	PT:LOC	LIKE	PT:PRO2SG
	Interpersonal			Predicator	
	(Did) you enjoy the party?				

J	Non-manual		head nod	
	Manual	PT:PRO1SG	LIKE	
	Interpersonal		Predicator	
	I enjoyed (it)			

J	Manual	BUT	HOME	PT:LOC	ARRIVE	LATE
	Interpersonal				Predicator	
	but (I) got back home late.					

Based on these three excerpts, it appears that the core paradigmatic distinction between [positive] and [negative] polarity is realized by a non-manual component: a movement of the signer's head in co-occurrence with the realization of the Predicator. A [negative] polarity is realized via a headshake; yet, there is optionality in the realization of [positive] polarity: there can be a head nod *or* no marked non-manual production, as demonstrated in the second and third clauses of Excerpt 3.10. This appears to align with systemic functional perspectives on language typology: [positive] clauses are less marked than their [negative] equivalents (Matthiessen, Teruya and Lam, 2010). Also, within sign linguistics literature (e.g., Pfau and Bos, 2016), a binary categorization of polarity is proposed typologically for sign languages: manual dominant languages (wherein polarity is realized via negative signs or particles) and non-manual dominant languages (wherein polarity is realized via the head and/or other non-manual components). As it is currently understood, BSL falls into the category of non-manual dominant sign languages with regard to marking negation, with non-manual components, particularly a headshake in the transverse plane, realizing this.

Nevertheless, such 'dominance' does not mean that other productive elements are excluded from this discussion on POLARITY. In fact, there are at least three other aspects that require consideration: the manual signs YES and NO; signs that phonologically alter to represent a change in polarity (usually from [positive] to [negative], e.g. HAVE-NOT); and the use of a clause-final headshake with a 'held' sign. These will be discussed in turn.

The extracts provided so far in this chapter have, in one way or another, demonstrated the way in which a clause may realize a binary selection in a system of POLARITY. In each case, the core element has concerned Predicator function, and the confirmation or refutation of the content of a previous move usually includes the manual repetition of the Predicator. The realization of the Predicator is thereby proposed to realize a major clause in interpersonal terms. However, individual manual signs representing YES and NO have been observed in recent usage-based investigations of BSL (Fenlon et al., 2014b). While these signs do not realize a Predicator function *per se*, they do provide responses to [interrogative] clauses and, even if used on their own, can present a move in the dialogue. As suggested in Excerpts 3.11 and 3.12, the sole use of YES and NO appears to act similarly to the kinds of 'minor clause' found in English, in that 'they serve to ensure the continuity of the interaction by supporting the current speaker's turn' (Halliday and Matthiessen, 2014, p.197):

[3.11]

B	**Non-manual**		brow raise	
	Manual	ALCOHOL	DRINK	PT:PRO2SG
	Interpersonal		Predicator	
		(Do) you drink alcohol?		

A	**Non-manual**	headshake
	Manual	NO
		No.

[3.12]

A	**Non-manual**			brow raise	
	Manual	-s-a-m-	PT:PRO3SG	KNOW	PT:PRO2SG
	Interpersonal			Predicator	
		(Do) you know Sam?			

B	**Non-manual**	head nod		
	Manual	YES		
		Yes,		

B	**Manual**	PT:PRO3SG	MEET	BEFORE
	Interpersonal		Predicator	
		(I) met him before.		

The manual signs used in Excerpts 3.11 and 3.12 are shown in Figure 3.6, but it must be remembered that there are several other signs in contemporary usage that can realize [positive] and [negative] polarity in a similar fashion. Online dictionaries such as the BSL Signbank (Fenlon et al., 2014a) demonstrate these in further detail, along with other potential glosses such as DENIAL, NOT and REFUSE.

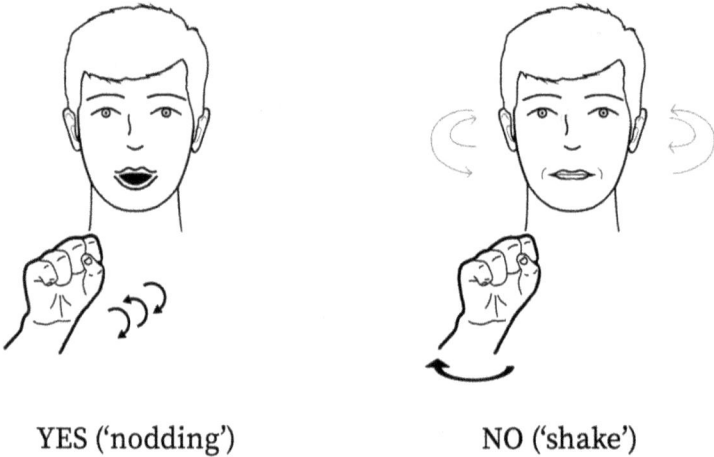

YES ('nodding')   NO ('shake')

Figure 3.6 Ways of signing YES and NO in BSL.

Other signs in BSL exist that realize [negative] polarity within themselves, including NOT-YET and NOT-MATTER. Certain 'positive' signs may also be modified in their production to express a 'negated' counterpart meaning. This can be observed, for instance, in the pairs WANT/NOT-WANT – the former with the dominant hand arcing down and away from the signer's chest, and the latter arcing up and away from the signer's chest – and TRUE/NOT-TRUE – the former with the dominant hand contacting the palm of the non-dominant hand, and the latter doing the same and then 'sweeping' across and away from the non-dominant hand (see Figure 3.7). The headshake co-occurs with these 'negative' counterparts (and this does not lead to a double negative situation as seen in English).

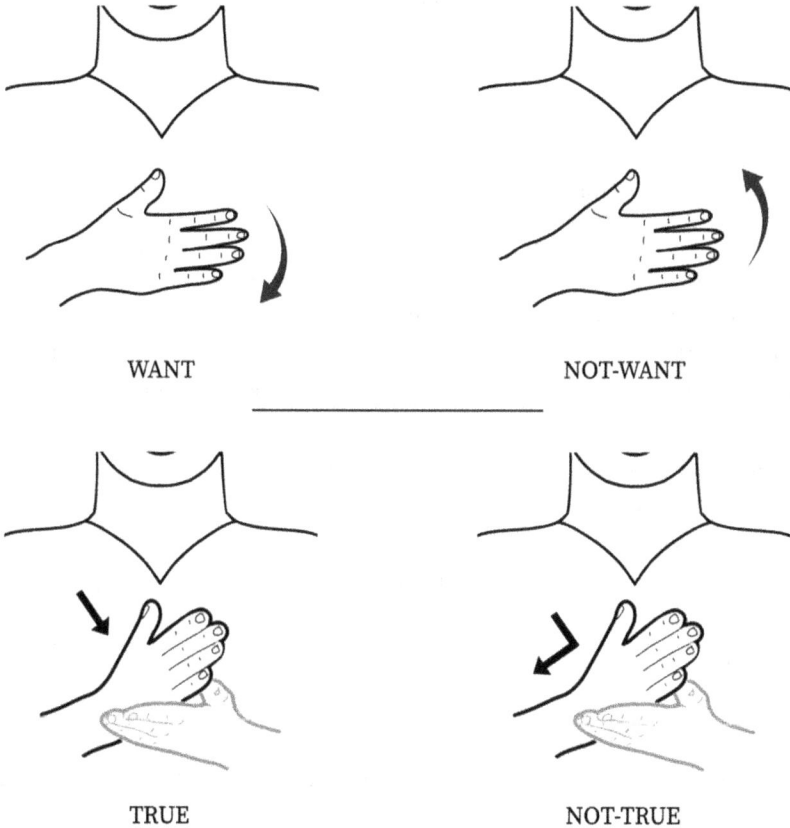

Figure 3.7 The polarity pairs of WANT/NOT-WANT and TRUE/NOT-TRUE in BSL.

Also observed in the dataset were instances of [negative] polarity realized by a non-manual headshake co-occurring with the Predicator function, but incorporating further prosodic effects. Excerpt 3.13 demonstrates an example of this:

[3.13]

S				
	Non-manual	brow raise		headshake
	Manual	LAST-YEAR	HOLIDAY	CHEAP
	Interpersonal			Predicator
		Last year's holiday (was) not cheap.		

```
                                              ┌─ negative
                                              │  ↘ +head shake;
major clause        POLARITY                  │     Predicator/head shake
   ↘ + Predicator   ──────────────▶           │
                                              └─ positive
```

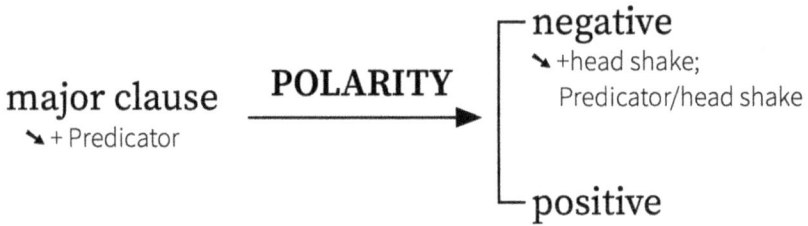

Figure 3.8 BSL system of POLARITY.

S states in Excerpt 3.13 that the cost of a holiday was expensive, but the clause is signed with raised eyebrows throughout, as if realizing an [interrogative: polar] selection. However, the production of CHEAP is held in mid-air as the eyebrows return to a neutral position and the headshakes. From the perspective of POLARITY, this is another instance in which a [negative] option can be chosen, such that the final headshake 'scopes backwards' and is applicable to the earlier information presented in the clause. This effect appears to be an interaction between interpersonal and textual elements, specifically altering the prominence of certain elements of the clause, and will be returned to in Chapter 5.

This brief exploration of POLARITY in BSL indicates that there is an overall distinction that can be made between [positive] and [negative] selections, schematized to a low level of delicacy in Figure 3.8. The realization of choices is complex and shows, like MOOD, that there are several resources within the visual-spatial modality that can be used. While this complexity is particularly broad in terms of [negative] choices at clause level, the general linking factor appears to be the use of a headshake co-occurring with the Predicator function.

MODALITY

The previous section demonstrated how [positive] and [negative] polarity can be realized, but this is not to say that this binary opposition is void of an in-between. It is within this 'neither here nor there' space that MODALITY appears, otherwise understood as those 'expressions of indeterminacy between the positive and negative poles, which interpersonally construct the semantic region of uncertainty' (Matthiessen et al., 2010, p.141). It is also within this area that expressions of probability and obligation are observed.

As with previous interpersonal systems, MODALITY involves more than just elements that are produced manually. Excerpt 3.14 demonstrates such an instance:

[3.14]

L	**Non-manual**					head tilt; narrow eyes
	Manual	NEXT-WEEK	PT:PRO1SG	SEE	FILM	MAYBE
	Interpersonal			Pred.		Modal

Maybe I (will) see a film next week.

L's statement, unlike the excerpts seen so far in this chapter, expresses information alongside a sign that blurs the possibility of this information being acted upon. This is performed using MAYBE, more or less conveying the same notion of probability or uncertainty as is understood in English, and is designated here as realizing a Modal function. Additionally, the non-manual tier shows that L uses a head tilt on the coronal plane and a narrowing of the eyes (see Figure 3.9). This non-manual production does not need to be produced with MAYBE to realize probability or uncertainty, but it assists in grading the desired force of the statement being made.

MAYBE

Figure 3.9 MAYBE in BSL with additional non-manual production.

In some instances, certain manual signs realizing a Modal function conflate with other functions, particularly that of the Predicator, as shown in Excerpts 3.15 and 3.16:

[3.15]

J	Non-manual				brow raise
	Manual	NOW	PT:PRO2SG	DRIVE	CAN
	Interpersonal				Predicator/Modal

Can you drive yet?

M	Non-manual		headshake	
	Manual	CAN-NOT		PT:PRO1SG
	Interpersonal	Predicator/Modal		

I cannot (drive).

[3.16]

M	Manual	PT:PRO3SG	APOLOGISE	SHOULD
	Interpersonal			Predicator/Modal

He should apologise.

J	Non-manual	head nod
	Manual	SHOULD
	Interpersonal	Predicator/Modal

(He) should (apologise).

In both Excerpts 3.15 and 3.16, a Modal function is realized and repeated in some way. In Excerpt 3.15, J wishes to ascertain if M has now learned to drive since their last interaction. J's use of CAN allows the addition of a meaning of permission and/or ability, and M's response consists of this sign (with a [negative] selection in POLARITY) and a self-referential point. In Excerpt 3.16, the statement from M that someone should apologize is agreed with by J who responds with only SHOULD and a head nod to confirm their agreement. In both excerpts, the focal point of the clause or the part that is most 'at risk' shifts to these signs realizing a Modal function. Like the Predicator function seen in previous excerpts, Modal functions in these environments are subject to repetition, negation and so on, rather than what would have been the Predicator had these Modal realizations have not been produced (i.e. DRIVE in Excerpt 3.15 and APOLOGISE in

Excerpt 3.16). Therefore, in instances where a Modal function is realized and carries a meaning of permission, ability or necessity, such as SHOULD, CAN, MUST, WILL and so on, the Modal function generally conflates with the Predicator function.

One further possible realization of a Modal function is also proposed here, although this is done so with the caveat that it is open to wider interpretation. This is due to the primarily non-manual realization of this function, rather than by a particular manual sign, and issues regarding non-manual multifunctionality (see Mapson, 2014, 2020). An example of this is demonstrated in Excerpt 3.17:

[3.17]

A	Non-manual				gaze shift; narrow eyes
	Spatio-kinetic				final sign position held
	Manual	SON	PT:POSS3SG	NOW	TWENTY-FIVE-YEARS-OLD
	Interpersonal				Predicator/Modal
		His/Her son (is) now 25, perhaps.			

As A communicates of a piece of specific information, which happens to also realize the Predicator function in this clause, there is a change in non-manual and spatio-kinetic elements, including a narrowing in A's eye aperture and the manual sign TWENTY-FIVE-YEARS-OLD being 'held' rather than the hands returning to a neutral space. While the manual tier does not include a sign encoding uncertainty, as was observed in Excerpt 3.14, the other parts of the production do arguably realize an interpersonal meaning – one of uncertainty in the validity of the information being given – and therefore falling into the realms discussed here.[8]

Accordingly, the system network for MODALITY can be schematized as presented in Figure 3.10, demonstrating two levels of delicacy. As with the system of POLARITY, this system is open to further development and modification as further BSL data is analysed. Nonetheless, in its current state, the Modal function

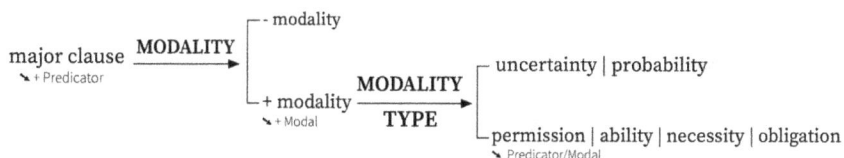

Figure 3.10 BSL system of MODALITY.

can be seen to be added to the clause when [+modality] is selected. The way in which Modal then operates, namely if it conflates with the Predicator function or if it operates independently, depends on the desired MODALITY TYPE. These secondary selections have been grouped in Figure 3.10, although the nuances in these selections are ready to be expanded upon from this point forward.

SOCIAL PROXIMITY

The final system presented in this chapter stands out from the previous systems despite its interpersonal nature. Whereas the systems of MOOD, POLARITY and MODALITY predominantly concern the message, its delivery and its overall 'certainty', SOCIAL PROXIMITY instead foregrounds the perceived, contextually bound relationship between the person communicating and those being communicated about, co-present or otherwise.

Similar systems in other languages have been posited. For instance, Teruya's (2007) description of Japanese includes the systems of POLITENESS and HONORIFICATION. These simultaneous systems impact the realization of the Predicator function with regard to contextual formality and culturally influenced manners of address – honorific, neutral or humble – relevant to those in communication (i.e. depending on their position within a social hierarchy). Other languages also have strategies for realizing similar hierarchies of formality, including the pronominal distinctions of *tú/usted* in Spanish and *tu/vous* in French (and their resultant effect on the realization of Predicator functions).

Distinctions such as these are also present in BSL, albeit a generally under-investigated part of the language (cf. Zeshan, 2000 for similar effects in Indo-Pakistani Sign Language (IPSL) and Barberà, 2014 for similar effects in LSC). Based on the dataset used for this chapter and data observed in previous works (e.g. Rudge, 2018), the realization of such hierarchical information appears to be optional. However, it is modality-specific in its realization; it requires distinctions in spatio-kinetic elements to be successfully communicated. An example of this is given in Excerpt 3.18, in which the topic of conversation involves memories of school life:

[3.18]

M	Non-manual					head nod
	Spatio-kinetic			high plane		high plane
	Manual	PT:POSS1SG	TEACHER	PT:PRO3SG	NICE	PT:PRO3SG
	Interpersonal				Predicator	

My teacher (was) nice.

M	Non-manual		
	Spatio-kinetic	high plane	high to mid plane
	Manual	PT:PRO3SG ALWAYS	$_{3SG}$-HELP-$_{1SG}$
	Interpersonal		Predicator
		She always helped me.	

M	Non-manual	brow raise; low-angled gaze	
	Manual	CD:[PT:PRO2SG	OKAY]
	Interpersonal		Predicator
		'(Are) you okay?'	

In Excerpt 3.18, M refers to a teacher that they remember. In doing so, they point to the referent's location in signing space, but the vertical height of the direction of the point is higher than elsewhere in M's dialogue (noted in the spatio-kinetic tier as 'high plane'). The second clause shows the point repeated at the higher vertical level, followed by the verb sign HELP, the start and end positions of which can be used to identify the one giving the help and the one receiving the help. This sign begins at the location of TEACHER and moves from this higher point down to a mid or 'neutral' level in front of the signer's chest. In the third clause, M employs constructed dialogue to take on the role of the teacher in question and sign as if from the teacher's perspective. Albeit brief, the clause includes the use of a downwards eye gaze as if asking the question from 'above'.

There appears to be three broad heights of vertical planes of reference, as presented in Figure 3.11. Referents placed in the high plane seem to refer to entities that are higher in a social hierarchy (wherein the signer is 'subordinate') and those placed in the low place seem to refer to entities that are lower in a social hierarchy (wherein the signer is 'superior'). Referents placed in the mid-plane are thus viewed as social equals.

The intricacy of this phenomenon seems to stretch a little further, however, as demonstrated in M's final clause. During M's constructed dialogue, the direction of M's eye gaze towards the lower vertical plane realizes a social hierarchy dissimilar from the first two clauses: M is signing in the guise of the teacher, and the teacher is 'superior' to the imagined referents being asked the question. As such, the roles that a signer can shift into can also encode this social proximity from the perspective of the role at the time. Consequently, when schematized into a system network, SOCIAL PROXIMITY (see Figure 3.12) includes the different

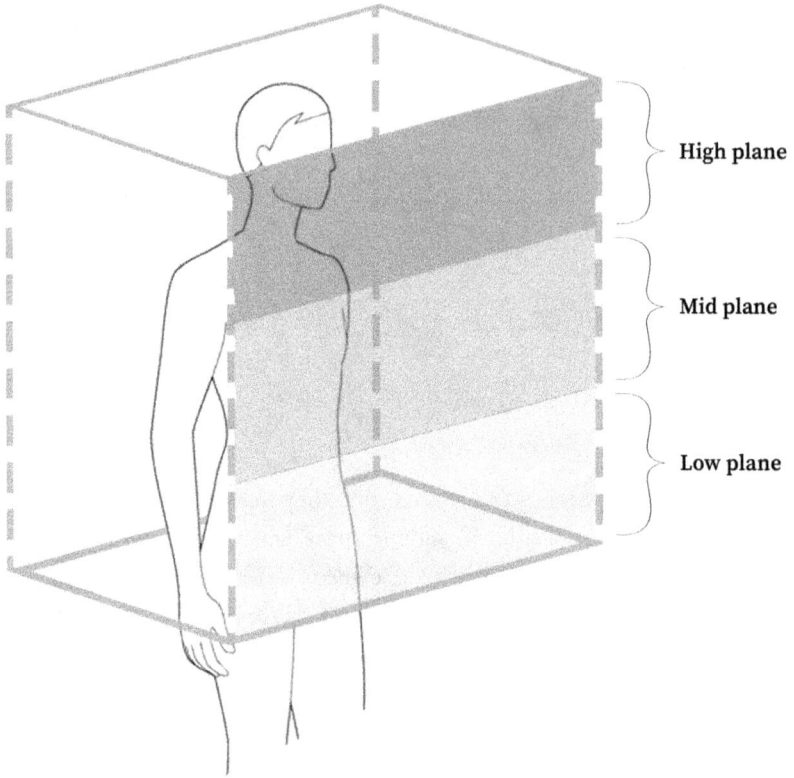

Figure 3.11 Broad indications of 'vertical planes' in BSL production.

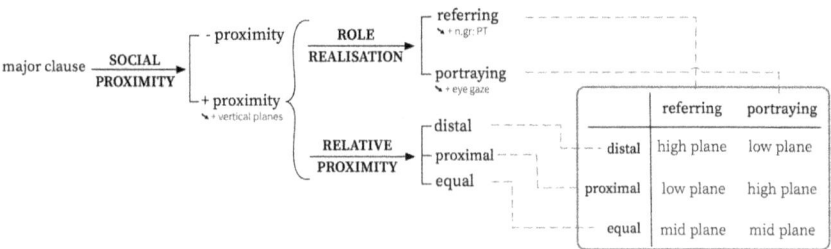

Figure 3.12 BSL system of SOCIAL PROXIMITY.[9]

combinations of directions of points and/or non-manual components towards the three vertical planes, and how these may differ depending on whether the realization of the role is via reference or portrayal.

Although this use of vertical height to realize interpersonal meaning is noted to occur in BSL, IPSL and LSC, it must also be viewed with some caution. This is due to the difficulty in distinguishing between a signer's use of topographic (imagined physical) and arbitrary (grammatical) signing space, as discussed in Chapter 1 (see also Cormier, Fenlon and Schembri, 2015). For instance, in topographic space, using different vertical planes of reference can indicate physical aspects such as a height difference between the signer and the referent. Consequently, referring to a small animal on the floor would result in a pointing sign directed towards the low plane, thus making it more likely that the physical trait is being expressed (i.e. closer to experiential meaning) rather than interpersonal aspects of superiority and subordination. Each possible instance of SOCIAL PROXIMITY therefore needs to be analysed within its context and co-text to reach a reasoned conclusion. Two further anecdotal instances of the use of the high plane have been observed: a signer referring to their manager using the high plane (despite prior knowledge that this person was considerably shorter than the signer) and when large entities such as the UK's National Health Service have been referred to, they can sometimes be referred to on the high place, indicating that they are socially 'dominant'.

The interpersonal networks of BSL

The system networks discussed in this chapter can be combined into a larger network demonstrating their simultaneous nature. Figure 3.13 shows the primary interpersonal systems of MOOD, POLARITY, MODALITY and SOCIAL PROXIMITY together.

It is now possible to observe how these systems operate in tandem and how selections are made within an extended exchange. Excerpt 3.19 presents dialogue between S and L (from the same dataset as previous excerpts in this chapter) who are discussing forthcoming holidays. Each clause has been split into its own glossed line (fifteen in total, indicated by roman numerals i to xv) and carries its own interpersonal analysis, displaying non-manual and spatio-kinetic tiers where appropriate.

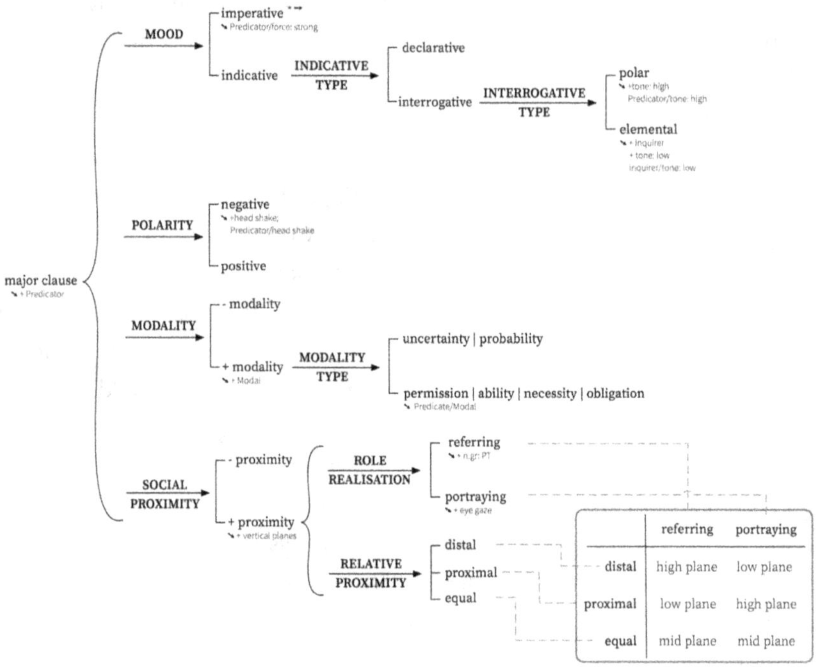

Figure 3.13 The interpersonal systems of BSL.

[3.19]

i	S	**Non-manual**		brow raise
		Manual	HOLIDAY	NEXT-WEEK
		Interpersonal		Predicator

(Is your) holiday next week?

ii	L	**Non-manual**	head nod
		Manual	NEXT-WEEK
		Interpersonal	Predicator

(Yes, it's) next week.

iii	L	**Manual**	FAMILY WITH CORNWALL PT:LOC		GO
		Interpersonal			Predicator

(I am) going with family to Cornwall.

iv	S	**Manual**	CORNWALL	NICE
		Interpersonal		Predicator

Cornwall (is) nice.

v	S	Non-manual			head nod
		Manual	BEACH	PT:LOC	LOVELY
		Interpersonal			Predicator

The beach (is) lovely.

vi	L	Non-manual					squinted eyes; puffed cheeks
		Manual	BUT	PEOPLE	PT:LOC	ALWAYS	DC:MANY-PEOPLE-CONGREGATE
		Interpersonal					Predicator

But there (are) always so many people!

vii	L	Manual	PT:PRO1SG	WEATHER	LOVE
		Interpersonal			Predicator

I love the weather,

viii	L	Non-manual			strong head nod; squinted eyes
		Manual	BUT	CROWD	HATE
		Interpersonal			Predicator

but (I) hate the crowds!

(Short pause between clauses)

ix	L	Non-manual			brow furrow
		Manual	PT:PRO2SG	HOLIDAY	WHAT
		Interpersonal			Predicator/Inquirer

What (about) your holiday?

x	S	Non-manual		headshake
		Manual	PT:PRO1SG	NOTHING
		Interpersonal		Predicator

I (have) nothing planned.

xi	S	Manual	HOLIDAY	DIFFICULT
		Interpersonal		Predicator

(Taking) holiday (is) difficult

xii S	Non-manual				head nod
	Spatio-kinetic			high plane	
	Manual	WHY	BOSS	PT:PRO3SG	STRICT
	Interpersonal				Predicator

because (my) manager (is) very strict.

xiii L	Non-manual		head nod
	Manual	COMPLAIN	SHOULD
	Interpersonal		Predicator/Modal

(You) should complain.

xiv S	Non-manual	head nod
	Manual	SHOULD
	Interpersonal	Predicator/Modal

(I) should (complain),

xv S	Non-manual		grimace
	Manual	BUT	NERVOUS
	Interpersonal		Predicator

but (I'm) really nervous.

Overall, the dialogue demonstrates that interpersonal meanings tend to be located, or are more 'at risk', towards the end of a clause. In each of the fifteen clauses presented here (and in most of the excerpts presented in this chapter), the Predicator function and/or the non-manual components that phonologically realize choices in systems like MOOD are realized as the final element in the clause. This, of course, does not mean to say that interpersonal meaning will always be towards the end of a clause, but observed trends suggest that this will generally be the case.

In terms of MOOD, most clauses – thirteen out of fifteen – realize a [declarative] selection, with only (i) and (ix) realizing [interrogative: polar] and [interrogative: elemental], respectively. Clauses realizing [interrogative] selections are logically followed by the other signer responding with [declarative] clauses, but turns between signers may then switch via [declarative] clauses, such as when a complementary viewpoint (as in (iv)) or an adversative viewpoint (as in (vi)) is offered.

Looking at clause (ix) in closer detail, a conflation of Predicator and Inquirer functions is noted. After a brief pause in the dialogue, L attempts to shift the focus of the conversation to S, still on the topic of holidays but more precisely on S's plans (via the use of a point towards S, i.e. PT:PRO2SG). This short clause juxtaposes two nominal groups and does not involve an overt verb sign or a verb group. As is discussed in this chapter, and as will be explored in more detail in Chapter 4, clauses such as these are permissible moves and tend to follow the pattern that the latter part of the clause – the Predicator, from interpersonal perspectives – further defines, describes or delimits the element that comes before it. In clause (ix), the information defining or describing PT:PRO2SG HOLIDAY is unknown to L, and this is thus indicated with an appropriate realization of the Inquirer function: WHAT.

From the perspective of POLARITY, all but one clause realizes a [positive] selection. Clause (x) indicates a [negative] selection in the system through the expression of a non-manual headshake in co-occurrence with NOTHING, which in turn realizes the Predicator function. However, there are also variations in the realization of positive selections throughout the excerpt: unmarked in (xi); marked with a head nod in (v) and marked with additional force as in (viii).

There are two clauses that realize a Modal function (i.e. all other clauses select for [- modality] in MODALITY). In clause (xiii), L suggests that S should complain about the manager in question for not being easy to reason with concerning time off work. L signs SHOULD, suggesting obligation on S's part, which is repeated and confirmed by S in clause (xiv). This also shows another conflation of the Predicator function, this time with the Modal function, which is suggested in the system network given the sense of obligation encoded within SHOULD.

Finally, in terms of SOCIAL PROXIMITY, clause (xii) demonstrates an instance where [+ proximity] is selected in the network. In this case, S refers to their manager in two steps: the identification of who the referent is by the fully lexical sign BOSS and the placement of their referent in signing space using a pointing sign. The latter is placed within the high plane, as indicated in Figure 3.11, indicating that S wishes to make known the nature of their social relationship (i.e. via selections of [+ proximity: distal] and [+ proximity: referring]).

Summary

This chapter began stating that cooperation is a vital factor in the range of potential communicative contexts in which we find ourselves, and that language can be viewed as a conduit for the negotiation of meanings made and stances taken between those in communication. Via the analysis and explanation of instances of dialogic interaction in BSL, the systems of MOOD, POLARITY, MODALITY and

SOCIAL PROXIMITY have been presented. For those readers who have experience in systemic functional typology or knowledge of systemic functional descriptions of spoken languages, this chapter should demonstrate that there are similarities at these relatively low levels of delicacy (e.g. the organization of MOOD, the binary options in POLARITY and so on). However, the visual-spatial modality allows for realizations of these choices that go beyond just the manual sign, and given the prosodic nature of the interpersonal metafunction, it is perhaps not surprising that the system of VISUAL PROSODY in the phonological stratum is implicated extensively, coupled with the gradient (rather than discrete) nature of these realizations.

The interpersonal metafunction within BSL is a complex area, with many research routes now available to expand on and challenge. For ease of reference, a summary of these areas of exploration is available in Chapter 7. For now, though, our focus turns to the experiential metafunction.

Exploring the Experiential Metafunction

The previous chapter presented one perspective of how meaning can be made in BSL, namely, the way in which meaning is negotiated or exchanged between users of the language. This permitted an understanding of how interaction can commence and be continued via core interpersonal functions realized within a BSL clause. With that in mind, a complementary level of understanding can now be explored: what can be said about the specific content of those exchanges? Chapter 3 demonstrated that the Predicator function is vital in allowing the 'back and forth' of a conversation in BSL, but it did not identify the topics or themes that BSL users were communicating about. However, from an experiential perspective, it is possible to analyse and explain how we deal with the what's, how's, when's and so on of our day-to-day experiences.

This chapter begins by briefly overviewing the experiential metafunction in relation to aspects of context and discourse semantics (i.e. identifying the metafunction axially from above and from roundabout). The contextual area of field is explored with regard to how experiences can be schematized and categorized into domains, which are then connected to the discourse semantic system of IDEATION and its relation to defining instances or 'quanta' of experience. Following this, the lexicogrammatical stratum is explored in depth. Using analysed examples of clauses produced by BSL users, a basic experiential grammar of BSL is proposed. This experiential grammar focuses on the system of TRANSITIVITY: Process types (relating to domains of experience); Participants (relating to the roles of those involved in these Processes); and Circumstances (relating to peripheral information expressed within the clause). The different system networks explored in this chapter are then brought together to form a larger experiential network, with selections made within this network exemplified via an analysis of extended BSL discourse.

Whereas excerpts in Chapter 3 showed that not all elements of a BSL clause realize an interpersonal function, experiential perspectives generally identify a more extensive set of functions that are realized across clauses. Furthermore, given the productive capabilities of BSL noted in Chapters 1 and 2 – specifically, the opportunities for productive simultaneity afforded by multiple articulators – there are instances where functional components may be 'repeated' in the same clause but not necessarily in the same form. For instance, an entity introduced by a fully lexical sign may be again referred to in the same clause by different (non-)manual elements, in turn leading to questions on typical experiential clause analyses and how these 'repeated' elements might be best addressed.

Prior to commencing, a brief reminder is required. It was noted in Chapter 2 that there are three core metafunctions from systemic functional perspectives: the interpersonal, the ideational and the textual, with the second of these metafunctions composed of experiential and logical subtypes. As the name of this chapter suggests, and as has been discussed so far, the focus here is on the experiential side of the broader ideational metafunction, rather than the logical side. The primary reason for this is to enable easier comparison with the interpersonal and textual analyses offered in this work: the systems presented in this book have the clause simplex (i.e. individual clauses and their internal composition) as the point of departure for the realization of interpersonal, experiential and textual meanings. Conversely, the logical metafunction is concerned with the clause complex (i.e. combinations of two or more clauses and their logico-semantic relationships, such as expansion, projection and so on; see Chapter 7 of Halliday and Matthiessen, 2014). The clause complex in BSL and the complexing of other lexicogrammatical ranks (e.g. group) are, of course, involved in making meaning, but these go beyond the scope of the present work.

Enabling experience

The ideational metafunction is covered in extensive detail in works such as Halliday and Matthiessen (1999). This section will briefly overview some of its core points to frame the remainder of the chapter and the analysis of experiential meanings in BSL. As with Chapter 3, this starts by considering the experiential metafunction from above (i.e. contextually).

From above, the region of contextual interest is field. This part of context generally covers variables regarding the activities being performed via either language (e.g. telling a fantasy story to a group of children) or alongside language (e.g. verbally guiding someone into a parking space). Contextual field is more specifically understood as the area concerning 'culturally recognized repertoires of social practices and concerns' (Halliday and Matthiessen, 1999, p.320) that may be split into first-order (activity) and second-order (subject matter) varieties. Given the wide potential of experiences and activities, particularly those that call on semiotic resources or that can be communicated via a semiotic resource (e.g. sharing, exploring or, more generically, 'doing'; see Matthiessen, Teruya and Canzhong, 2008), field has an understandably vast scope. This includes but is not limited to notions of institutionalization (i.e. any narrow or broad expectations of communications within a certain sociocultural context), topics that are implicated within the domain of experience, and individual participant knowledge in the interactions (Leckie-Tarry, 1995).

The intricacies of this metafunction extend into observations when viewed from roundabout (i.e. at the discourse semantic stratum). Halliday and Matthiessen (1999) note that 'the semantic correlate of a contextual field is a domain' (p.323), wherein a domain consists of 'the ideational meanings that are "at risk"' (ibid.). Put briefly, domains of experience are rooted in four core experiences: doing, being, sensing and expressing.[1] These can be combined in various ways to result in common sub-domains, which may in turn be combined and refined further to more specific actions or states, and so on. Figure 4.1 (adapted from Halliday and Matthiessen, 1999, 2014) presents a visual interpretation of these broad combinations which, while not completely holistic, attempt to demarcate a space of semiotic and experiential potential.

When dealing with the discourse semantic components of the domains of experience, the broadest category is that of *phenomena*: 'anything that can be construed as part of a human experience' (Halliday and Matthiessen, 1999, p.48). Phenomena can be split into sequences, figures and elements. Figure 4.2 summarizes this via an adapted version of Halliday and Matthiessen's (1999) more elaborate system of IDEATION. It also includes initial lexicogrammatical considerations: figures and elements are realized at clause rank or below, whereas sequences are realized by clause complexes and the relationships between them (and, as indicated above, are not of immediate concern in the current work).

The figure is viewed experientially as a base unit of interaction, somewhat analogous to the interpersonal 'move' discussed in Chapter 3. Halliday and Matthiessen (1999) identify that 'the key to the construal of experience is the perception of change' (p.213) with the figure acting as this 'basic fragment of experience that embodies one quantum of change [...] – it is a constellation of actors and props; and it unfolds through time' (p.128). For instance, the following is a figure realized in English: *Justine informed the police last night.* This figure's 'quantum of change' is an action of passing information between two parties at a certain time. Three semantic elements are noted: a Process as the central element of the figure (of which six overall types are identified on the outer limits of Figure 4.1); two Participants taking part in the Process of the figure; and a Circumstance that refines the figure further. In terms of elements, then, the above example has the Process realized as *informed*, the Participants as *Justine* and *the police*, and a Circumstance of *last night*. The core of this figure (the Process) necessitates the inclusion of those involved in the action (the Participants), but sense would be maintained should the temporal information be excluded (i.e. the Circumstance *last night* can be omitted without impacting the integrity of the figure, but omitting the Participant *the police* would result in an incomplete figure). In terms of discourse semantic elements, then, this core Process needs its two Participants for complete realization of the experience, but the Circumstance is not mandatory.

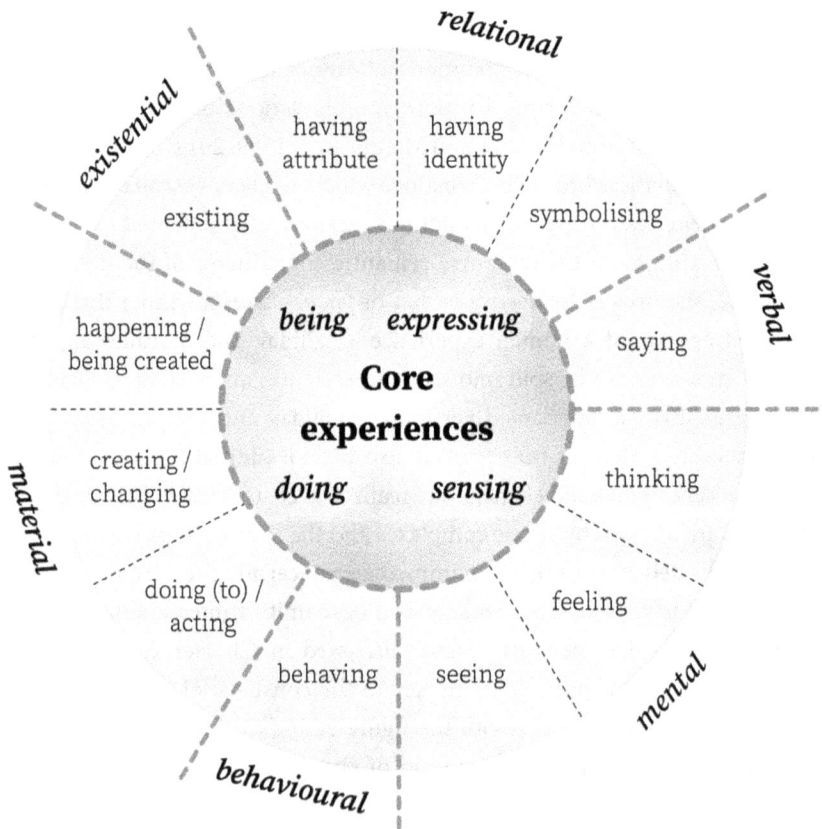

Figure 4.1 Domains of broad and combined experience, adapted from Halliday and Matthiessen (1999, 2014).

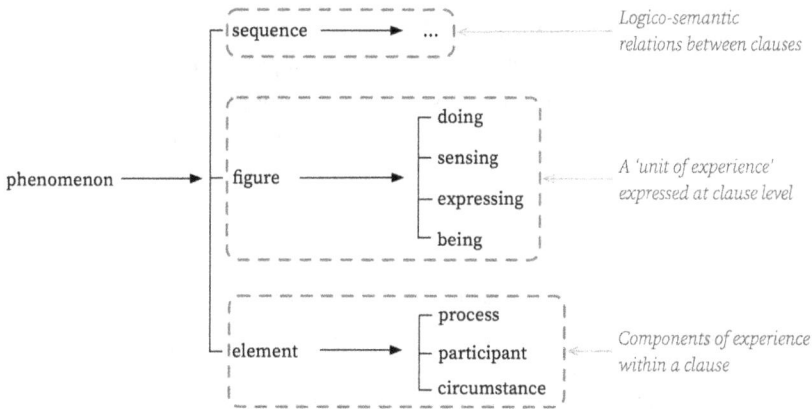

Figure 4.2 The discourse semantic system of IDEATION.

While the above gives introductory insight into understanding the experiential metafunction at the discourse semantic stratum, its complexity is far greater. What has been discussed so far has offered one of two 'models of participation' (Halliday and Matthiessen, 1999, p.149) concerning the interpretation of experience, known as the transitivity model (i.e. diversifying experience into domains and sub-domains). The second model, ergativity, instead attempts to unify experiences across domains by identifying, for example, commonalities in agency across experiences. While this latter model is certainly worth exploration, the transitivity model is the one focused on in this chapter, implicating the lexicogrammatical system of TRANSITIVITY.

Towards an experiential grammar of BSL

TRANSITIVITY concerns the lexicogrammatical realizations of the above mentioned components within IDEATION (i.e. figures and elements). There are two systems that are discussed from this point forward: PROCESS TYPE and CIRCUMSTANCE. PROCESS TYPE concerns realizations of both Process elements (see the outer edge of Figure 4.1) and Participant elements given their strong interdependency, as exemplified in the previous section. CIRCUMSTANCE discusses realizations of the more peripheral elements of Circumstance. The entry condition for these simultaneous lexicogrammatical systems is the major clause, as was seen with MOOD in Chapter 3.

Exploring British Sign Language

Prior to observing these systems in further detail, it is sensible to revisit the impact of productive simultaneity of BSL expression on linguistic analysis and description. From an experiential perspective, the potential of simultaneously using manual, non-manual and visual-spatial resources has a considerable impact. To exemplify this point, a comparative example between English and BSL using a rudimentary transitivity analysis is presented in Excerpt 4.1a:

[4.1a]

English	Both people	walked	side-by-side
Experiential	Participant	Process	Circumstance

The analysis of Excerpt 4.1a shows what would be expected based on previous explanations of the experiential figure: there is a core or nuclear Process indicating action or state (*walked*), a Participant indicating who or what is involved in the action (*both people*) and an optional manner in which the action was performed (*side-by-side*). An equivalent clause in BSL is presented in Excerpt 4.1b, with Figure 4.3 showing the stages of BSL production of this clause:

[4.1b]

BSL	PEOPLE BOTH	DC:TWO-PEOPLE-WALK-SIDE-BY-SIDE
Experiential	Participant	Process | Participant | Circumstance

The Participant in Excerpt 4.1b is realized by two fully lexical manual signs (PEOPLE BOTH). However, a depicting construction (DC:TWO-PEOPLE-WALK-SIDE-BY-SIDE) is then used, incorporating a substantial level of productive simultaneity. This depicting construction realizes the Process of walking, the Circumstance of the side-by-side manner of walking and, through the use of the handshape, a 'repetition' of the Participant, produced in a different form to that seen in the preceding fully lexical signs.

At first glance, such productions might appear to be difficult to interpret and analyse from a systemic functional perspective. However, as initially proposed in Rudge (2018), depicting constructions such as these will have commonalities in terms of what the manual, non-manual and spatio-kinetic aspects can realize from experiential perspectives. The depicting construction of Excerpt 4.1b shown in Figure 4.3 is re-annotated in Figure 4.4 to identify which experiential functions are realized by which productive features. This also shows, in parentheses, that the head and the motion/displacement of the hands could also realize further circumstantial meaning (e.g. if Excerpt 4.1b were produced with the signer's tongue protruding to the side and with a meandering manual path of motion, this may suggest a clumsy or an inebriated manner of walking).

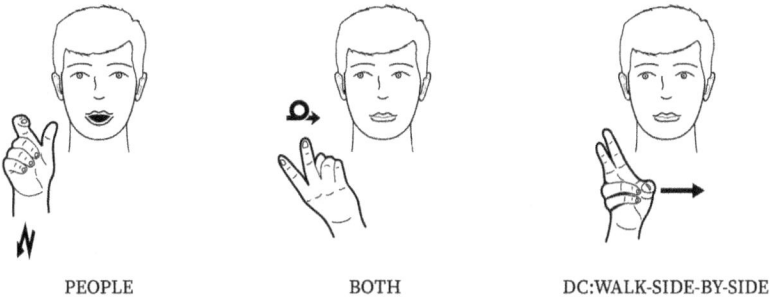

PEOPLE   BOTH   DC:WALK-SIDE-BY-SIDE

Figure 4.3 PEOPLE BOTH DC:TWO-PEOPLE-WALK-SIDE-BY-SIDE.

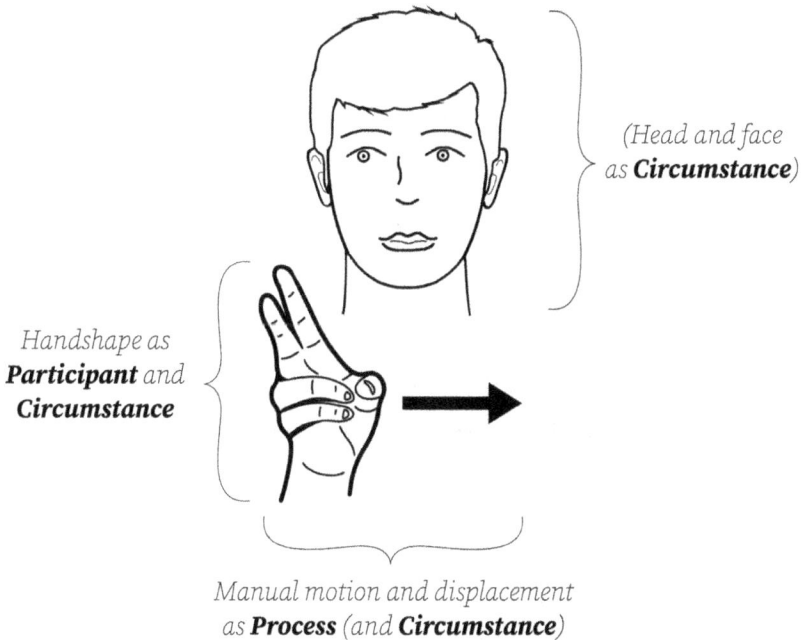

(Head and face as **Circumstance***)*

Handshape as **Participant** *and* **Circumstance**

Manual motion and displacement as **Process** *(and* **Circumstance***)*

Figure 4.4 Experiential functions and their correlates in depicting constructions.

With this simultaneity in mind, it is important to address the potential for 'duplicate' occurrences of functional components to appear, such as the Participant in Excerpt 4.1b. To more easily identify when a functional component appears more than once in a clause, the first or 'core' realization of the experiential function will appear in black, whereas any secondary/repeated productions will appear in grey, as demonstrated in Excerpt 4.1c:

[4.1c]

BSL	PEOPLE	BOTH	DC:TWO-PEOPLE-WALK-SIDE-BY-SIDE
Experiential	Participant		Process | Participant | Circumstance

The BSL data analysed for this chapter are drawn from a set of recorded instances of monologic narratives by BSL users. Prior to these recordings, BSL users were given time and prompts to think about two or three stories that they would be comfortable sharing on camera. As this was intended neither as a test of memory nor as fluency, signers were allowed to pause, repeat and restart as they wished, and could use prompts or notes if desired. Like the data analysed in Chapter 3, topics were not controlled, but signers were encouraged to include as much detail as possible (wherein any personally identifiable information has again been pseudonymized or redacted during analysis) to elicit as many different domains of experience as possible. Recordings took place one-by-one in a comfortably sized room, although participants were asked to sign directly towards a camera rather than a person. This more controlled setting is likely to have had an impact on the productions, but to attempt to mitigate this, the first few minutes of each recording was discarded from analysis.

Material processes

In the broadest sense, actions – things that we do or that are being done – are understood experientially as material Processes. These Processes 'construe doings [...] and happenings' (Matthiessen, Teruya and Lam, 2010, p.135) and are concerned with phenomena that occur in the outside world, such as grabbing or pushing, as opposed to those that may happen 'internally', such as thinking and reasoning. Material Processes may be realized in numerous ways in BSL, including both fully lexical signs (e.g. BUILD, DRAW, GROW, SKIP, WALK and CLOSE) and constructions that incorporate partly lexical signs (i.e. depicting constructions such as those presented in Excerpts 4.1b and 4.1c above). Each clause realizing a material Process also realizes at least one experiential Participant who performs the Process in question: the Actor. As such, there are two expected functions that are realized in any clause of this Process type: Process:material and Actor, as demonstrated in Excerpt 4.2:

[4.2]

H	**Manual**	PT:PRO1SG	DRIVE
	Experiential	Actor	Process:material
		I drive.	

As previously discussed, communication in the visual-spatial modality permits semiosis through means such as the space in front of a signer. This is a pertinent feature in terms of material Processes that incorporate actions of physical displacement, as this can often be represented via depicting constructions in BSL. Excerpt 4.3 offers one such example:

[4.3]

J	**Manual**	PT:POSS1SG DAUGHTER	DC:DAUGHTER-TURN-AROUND
	Experiential	Actor	Actor | Process:material
		My daughter turned around.	

In Excerpt 4.3, the signer uses a depicting construction to represent the previously identified Actor via an appropriate classifier handshape (i.e. an extended upright index finger to represent a human participant). By twisting the wrist so that the orientation of the palm faces towards the signer, the material Process of someone 'turning around' is communicated (see Figure 4.5). More complex movements and interactions between multiple Participants can also occur, as will be presented later, but it suffices for the moment to say that if the focus of the Process is one of a Participant's physical displacement, it may be realized via a depicting construction.

Similarly, a signer can also realize a material action via constructed action (or 'role shift'), as indicated in Excerpt 4.4:

[4.4]

J	**Non-manual**		furrowed brows; squinted eyes; head tilt (forward)
	Manual	PT:PRO3SG	CA:MARCHING
	Experiential	Actor	Actor | Process
		He marched.	

In Excerpt 4.4, J embodies the role of the Actor, mimetically performing the Process of 'marching'. The signer's feet do not move, so the signer is not

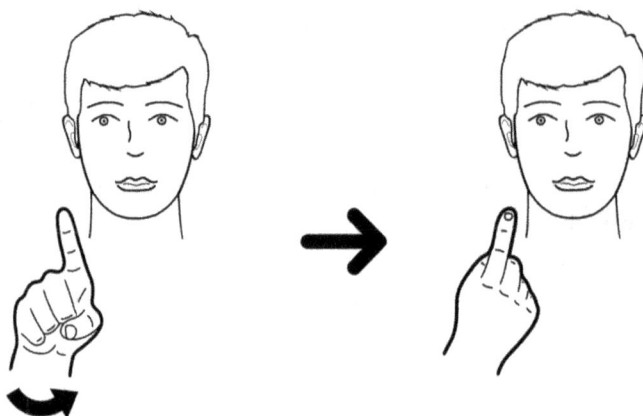

DC:DAUGHTER-TURN-AROUND

Figure 4.5 Two stages in the expression of DC:DAUGHTER-TURN-AROUND.

physically displacing themselves, and unlike a depicting construction, there is no specific handshape indicating a path or manner of displacement. Instead, J's upper body enacts the marching action of the Actor (i.e. arms bent at the elbow and swinging rhythmically) and also some Circumstantial information regarding the manner of the action via non-manual components (discussed in the following section on the system of CIRCUMSTANCE).

Therefore, the realization of a material Process may take one of three lexicogrammatical forms: fully lexical signs, depicting constructions and constructed action. The distinguishing functional factor between these three choices appears to be what the signer wishes to focus on regarding the action in question: if the focus is on physical displacement, a depicting construction is used; if the focus is on the specifics of the movement itself (including additional Circumstantial information), constructed action is used; otherwise, and if available in the BSL lexicon, a fully lexical sign is used.

Participants in clauses of material Processes can similarly vary in their function. So far, the above excerpts have included only the Actor as the 'doer' of the Process. When other Participants are involved in a clause, their functional role is based on meanings surrounding effects on said Participant(s) and the notion of benefaction.

Regarding Participant effects, Excerpts 4.5 and 4.6 demonstrate a primary distinction, specifically, whether Participants are impacted or modified in some manner by the Actor:

[4.5]

S	Manual	MOTHER	MEAT	COOK
	Experiential	Actor	Goal	Process:material

Mum cooked meat.

[4.6]

I	Manual	PT:PRO1SG	TENNIS	PLAY
	Experiential	Actor	Scope	Process:material

I play tennis.

Both Excerpts 4.5 and 4.6 demonstrate material Processes (COOK and PLAY) alongside Actors performing those actions (MOTHER and PT:PRO1SG). However, each excerpt also includes another Participant which functionally differs in its own context. In the case of Excerpt 4.5, MEAT is functionally ascribed as Goal as it is directly affected by the Actor (i.e. it is being directly prepared). Conversely, in Excerpt 4.6, while the Actor expresses their involvement in the Process of playing tennis, TENNIS itself is not directly affected or impacted by the Actor in such a way that MEAT is in Excerpt 4.5. As such, it operates functionally as a Scope, rather than a Goal. From what has been observed in the dataset pertaining to this chapter and in previous work (Rudge, 2018), configurations with Goal appear to be more common than those with Scope, but as material Processes can occur in BSL alongside Participants that are not directly impacted or affected, it is worthwhile to indicate this functional distinction.[2]

Another factor to consider in material Processes is the concept of benefaction. In certain instances, a distinction can be seen from the instances of 'effect' described above. In Excerpt 4.7, for example, a Participant 'benefits' from the material Process at hand.

[4.7]

S	Spatio-kin.			1 → 3
	Manual	GIFT	FRIEND PT:PRO3SG	GIVE
	Experiential	Goal	Recipient	Actor | Process:material | Recipient

I gave (my) friend a present.

S realizes three functional Participants: GIFT, FRIEND PT:PRO3SG and, via the signing space, the signer themselves, as indicated by GIVE starting from the signer and moving towards the location in signing space that FRIEND is located. As such, this clause realizes an Actor (the signer), a Goal (the present) and a beneficiary of the material Process (the friend), ascribed with the Recipient function (again, repeated via the ending location of the movement path for GIVE).

In terms of material Processes, then, a system network as shown in Figure 4.6 can be proposed. From the entry point of the major clause, a Process type is chosen (reduced in Figure 4.6 to [material] only, but this will be expanded on towards the end of the chapter). Both Actor and Process:material are inserted as functional components at the [material] selection, and then two simultaneous systems of MATERIAL FOCUS and MATERIAL PARTICIPANTS are available to select from. Selections in MATERIAL FOCUS will impact the lexicogrammatical realization of Process:material, and if there are two or more Participants in the clause, MATERIAL PARTICIPANTS can lead to the insertion of a Goal, a Scope and, potentially, a Recipient.

Mental and verbal Processes

While material Processes focus on experiences in the 'outer' world, both mental and verbal Processes are more closely associated with aspects of experience that are 'inner'. In other words, mental Processes concern aspects of consciousness and thought, and verbal Processes are concerned with moving the 'inner' to the 'outer' or, as Halliday and Matthiessen (2014) identify, the 'symbolic relationships constructed in human consciousness and enacted in the form of language' (p.215).

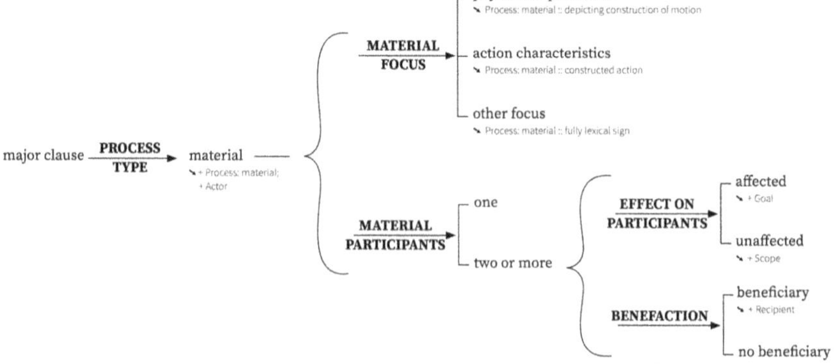

Figure 4.6 BSL systems for the material Process type.

Mental and verbal Processes are addressed under this same subheading as they are both capable of 'projection': a logico-semantic aspect using clause complexes to enable mental Process clauses to present ideas and thoughts (e.g. *I knew that he was lying*) and verbal Process clauses to present (in)direct locutions (e.g. *I said that you would enjoy it*). In fact, the similarities between these Process types are such that they share several system networks, although there are still sufficient differences between their functions and realizations in BSL to warrant their distinction. Excerpts 4.8 and 4.9 demonstrate simple clauses in these two experiential domains:

[4.8]

I	Manual	PT:PRO1SG	NUMBER	KNOW
	Experiential	Senser	Phenomenon	Process:mental
		I knew the number.		

[4.9]

J	Spatio-kinetic		3 → 1		
	Manual	PT:PRO3SG	TELL	RIGHT	RESPONSE
	Experiential	Sayer	Sayer | Process:verbal | Receiver	Verbiage	
		He told me the correct answer.			

In Excerpt 4.8, the mental Process KNOW requires a Participant to 'do the knowing', taking on the functional role of Senser. In this case, there is a specific thing that is known or more broadly 'sensed' by the Senser, which takes the role of Phenomenon (not to be confused with the entry condition of phenomenon in the discourse semantic system of IDEATION; see Figure 4.2). The Phenomenon is not necessarily required in such constructions, such that PT:PRO1SG KNOW (i.e. Senser and Process:mental) is also a permissible clause, with whatever associated Phenomenon either being unnecessary to state or recoverable from contextual/co-textual factors.

As with clauses realizing mental Processes, those realizing verbal Processes such as in Excerpt 4.9 also have a required Participant: Sayer.[3] In these constructions that semantically construe aspects in the communication domain, it is possible – but not necessary – to include what is said, taking the Participant role of Verbiage (somewhat analogous to the role of Phenomenon). However, clauses realizing verbal Processes permit additional Participants than what is seen accompanying mental Processes. In Excerpt 4.9, this is presented within TELL: the spatio-kinetic component of this verb sign indicates that the Sayer (in the third-person location in the signing space) communicates something to a Participant that can comprehend, respond to or acknowledge the communication (identified here as the signer themselves by PT:PRO1SG). This is ascribed the function of Receiver, forming an important point of distinction: mental Processes do not include additional analogous Participants to 'sense' a Phenomenon as (a) these cannot be transmitted from the Senser and (b) these Processes are inherently representations of 'inner' experience.

Nevertheless, as seen in Excerpt 4.10, certain verbal Process configurations do not include a Receiver despite a Participant being present that can 'receive':

[4.10]

I	**Spatio-kinetic**		$1 \rightarrow 3$
	Manual	PT:POSS3SG BROTHER	CONGRATULATE
	Experiential	Target	Sayer | Process:verbal | Target
		I congratulated my brother.	

In the case of Excerpt 4.10, the verbal act of congratulating by the Sayer (realized by the point in signing space to which the verb sign CONGRATULATE moves) results in the realization of a Target rather than a Receiver. This distinction is informed by Matthiessen, Teruya and Lam (2010), who state that a Target denotes 'the entity that is the object of judgement by the Sayer' (p.216). So, whereas in Excerpt 4.9 the comprehending Participant received new or confirmatory information, Excerpt 4.10 shows that the act of congratulating is the thing being 'received', thereby making these latter Sayer-Target constructions like the abovementioned Actor-Goal constructions found in material Process clauses. Nonetheless, verbal Processes involving a Target rather than a Receiver (i.e. in which the Sayer judges or evaluates another) are generally less frequent. Signs such as PRAISE, CONGRATULATE and BLAME result in this targeting configuration, although these tend to be generally less common than other signs such as SAY and SIGN.

It was noted above that both mental and verbal Processes can project in certain contexts. To elaborate further, in these instances, at least one additional clause is produced that takes on the Participant role of Phenomenon or Sayer for mental and verbal Processes, respectively. Excerpts 4.11 and 4.12 demonstrate instances of projection for both Process types:

[4.11]

S	Manual	PT:PRO1SG	THINK	PT:DET	BRILLIANT
	Experiential	Senser	Process:mental	Phenomenon	

I thought (that) that (was) brilliant.

[4.12]

J	Spatio-kinetic		3→ 1			
	Manual	PT:PRO3SG	TELL	PT:PRO3SG	SOON	MOVE
	Experiential	Sayer	Sayer | Process:verbal | Receiver	Verbiage		

He told me (that) he would move soon.

These two excerpts show how thoughts or communication may be reported. In both instances, both the Phenomenon and the Verbiage are composed of multiple elements which form a projected clause: the Phenomenon in Excerpt 4.11 is realized as a clause identifying a relational Process (explained in the following subsection) and the Verbiage in Excerpt 4.12 is an Actor (PT:PRO3SG) performing a material Process (MOVE) in a temporal Circumstance (SOON). The translations in each excerpt include *that* in parentheses to imply the similarity to using this subordinating conjunction to relate two clauses to one another.

A further form of projection is also observable, usually during instances where interactions between two or more people are reported by a single signer. Excerpt 4.13 shows a short example of where such an instance occurs:

[4.13]

I	Spatio-kinetic		gaze and torso left; raised eyebrows			
	Manual	PT:PRO3SG	CD:[BEEN	SEE	NEW	FILM]
	Experiential	Sayer	Verbiage			

She (asked/said to me) '(Have you) seen the new film?'

I	Spatio-kinetic		gaze and torso right; headshake	
	Manual	PT:PRO1SG	CD:[NOT-YET]	
	Experiential	Sayer	Verbiage	

I (responded) 'Not yet.'

In Excerpt 4.13, constructed dialogue is used by the signer to quote verbal content, firstly that of another Participant that had been previously identified in the discourse, and then that of their own discourse. In the excerpt, the change in direction of the eye gaze and torso are non-verbal cues denoting that the Participant attributed to the expressed Verbiage may not necessarily be the signer. In other words, the signer is no longer in 'narration mode' at this point and has instead adopted the role of the Sayer.

It is also worthwhile noting in Excerpt 4.13 that no overt verbal Process signs are realized, although adding this between the Sayer and the Verbiage (e.g. ASK or REPLY) would be permissible. In extended instances of constructed dialogue moving between multiple Sayers, signs realizing the Process in question can be ellipted because the use of constructed dialogue (in combination with preceding co-text) indicates the ongoing 'back and forth' between the Participants. Furthermore, the Sayer may also be ellipted in cases of frequent constructed dialogue sequences when individual Sayers are retrievable from the context, the preceding co-text or the non-manual features that are used by the signer, thereby leaving only the Verbiage overtly realized (see Cormier, Smith and Zwets, 2013, for an extended discussion on these combinations in extended narrative sequences in BSL).

With the above excerpts and explanations in mind, the system networks for mental and verbal Processes can now be schematized, shown in Figure 4.7. Unlike previous system networks displayed so far, these networks show a convergence point prior to the system of PROJECTION.[4] While mental Processes default directly to PROJECTION, verbal Processes can only access this system if the verbal activity of [disclosing] is selected (i.e. if the purpose of the verbal Process is to target, then there will be no Verbiage to express). Verbal Processes also have choices available in the system of RECEPTION depending on whether a secondary Participant in the figure is in receipt of what is expressed. Additionally, an if/

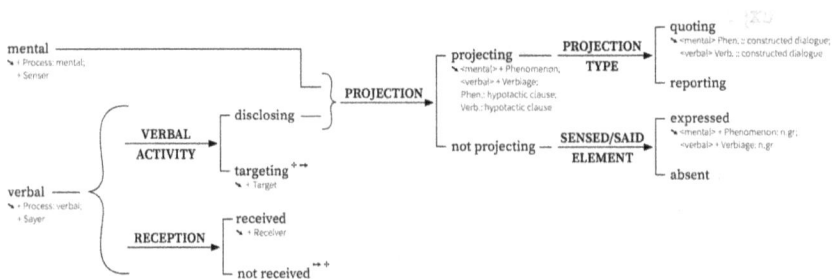

Figure 4.7 BSL systems for mental and verbal Process types.

then condition (indicated by the superscript symbols and arrows) is added for selections of [targeting] resulting in selections of [not received] (i.e. if the Sayer is verbally judging a Target, then a Receiver will likely not be present in the clause). At the point of PROJECTION, a binary choice is available. If [projecting], Phenomenon (for mental Processes) or Verbiage (for verbal Processes) will be included and take the form of a hypotactic clause which, if [quoting] rather than [reporting], will likely be realized as constructed dialogue. In instances of non-projection, it is still possible for Phenomenon or Verbiage to be realized, although these are expressed in nominal groups rather than hypotactic clauses. Finally, a selection of [absent] in the system of SENSED/SAID ELEMENT would result in a realization of only Process:mental and Senser or Process:verbal and Sayer. This may occur in instances where the content of what is sensed or expressed is deemed not important, but perhaps the manner of the action is. This is suggested in Excerpt 4.14 where the '++' indicates the partial or full manual repetition of a sign:

[4.14]

J	Manual	PT:PRO1SG	THINK++
	Experiential	Senser	Process:mental | Circumstance
		I thought for a while.	

Relational Processes

The experiences encompassed in the domain of relational Processes are those of 'being, having, and being at' (Matthiessen, Teruya and Lam, 2010, p.178). These can be primarily realized in languages such as English using the copula verb *to be*, such as *The bread is stale*, realizing a relational aspect of experience attributing an edible product to its current state of freshness. Relational constructions can be found in BSL clauses, but there are certain complexities that need to be elaborated on, the first of which can be exemplified in Excerpt 4.15:

[4.15]

S	Non-manual	raised eyebrows		head nod
	Manual	NEW	JOB	EXCITE
	Experiential	Index		Aspect
		(The) new job (is) exciting.		

S expresses a relationship between the two primary concepts: NEW JOB and EXCITE. This kind of relationship from functional perspectives would be understood as an intensive relational Process, wherein an element of experience is attributed with a value or a quality, assigned a group membership, and so on. In the case of Excerpt 4.15, and in most other intensive relational Process realizations in the current dataset, the element that is realized first in the clause – the Index – is ascribed the value or quality expressed afterwards – the Aspect.[5]

Unlike material, mental and verbal Processes, Excerpt 4.15 lacks the realization of an overt Process as a sign. Similarly, when viewed from group rank, a verbal group is not realized in this clause. The functional relationship between the Index and the Aspect thereby comes from their juxtaposition in the clause and a lack of a verbal group that would otherwise indicate the experiential relationship between the Participants. It can also be posited that certain non-manual features co-occur with these juxtapositions, wherein a marked change happens at the point where the signer finishes realizing the Index and begins realizing the Aspect. This has been noted in the non-manual tier of Excerpt 4.15, but it must nonetheless be considered cautiously: the use of raised eyebrows alongside the Index may be more appropriately related to textual functions such as Theme and Rheme (discussed in Chapter 5), and the head nod alongside the Aspect may be more appropriately ascribed to interpersonal concerns, such as (re)affirming the positive polarity of the move (discussed in Chapter 3).

Intensive relational Processes, however, are just one type found in BSL. These latter constructions realize the experience of 'being', and other relational Processes can indicate possession and the experience of 'having'. This is exemplified in Excerpt 4.16:

[4.16]

I	**Manual**	-p-e-t-e-	PT:PRO3SG	DOG	HAVE
	Experiential		Index	Aspect	Process:relational
		Pete has (a) dog.			

As relational Processes imply the existence of at least two Participants (i.e. to show the people, objects, things and phenomena that are in some sort of relationship), it is not surprising that both Index and Aspect are also found in Excerpt 4.16. However, unlike intensive relations, those of possession can use the overt verb sign HAVE to indicate that one Participant (the Aspect) is owned by or belongs to the other (the Index).[6] This also forms a point of distinction between relational Processes: if HAVE were omitted, leaving just the Index and

Aspect, the resulting meaning would be something equivalent to *Pete is a dog* (e.g. if 'Pete' had been previously mentioned and the signer was now disambiguating that the name refers to an animal rather than a human).

Further techniques for expressing possession are also possible in BSL, such as the use of pointing signs that are directed towards a Participant or location in the signing space, using a closed fist rather than an extended index finger (i.e. PT:POSS; see Figure 4.8). However, as demonstrated in Excerpt 4.17, this generally expresses possession within a nominal group, rather than across the clause:

[4.17]

S	Manual	PT:POSS1SG	HUSBAND	HAPPY
	Experiential	Index		Aspect
		My husband (was) happy.		

In Excerpt 4.17, possession is expressed within the realization of the Index (i.e. within the nominal group PT:POSS1SG HUSBAND) rather than having an overt verbal group that permits the realization of a possessive relational Process. Consequently, Excerpt 4.17 realizes an intensive relationship between an Index and an Aspect, as seen in Excerpt 4.15, although these nominal-level possessive structures are not restricted to relational Processes (e.g. PT:POSS1SG SON CRICKET PLAY – *My son plays cricket* – as an example of a material Process).

PT:PRO | PT:DET | PT:LOC   PT:POSS

Figure 4.8 Some differences in handshapes for pointing signs.

The third type of relational Process observed in BSL covers the experiential domain of 'being at' and is similar in structure to that of intensive relational Process clauses. The differentiating factor lies in the functional Aspect, as shown in Excerpt 4.18:

[4.18]

J	**Manual**	LESSON	EVERY	WEDNESDAY	MORNING
	Experiential	Index		Aspect/Circumstance	
	Lessons (were) every Wednesday morning.				

As with intensive relationships, Excerpt 4.18 does not realize an overt Process (i.e. the juxtaposition of the Index and the Aspect Participants fulfil the relational function) but the Aspect is conflated with Circumstantial information. Circumstantial elements within the experiential metafunction are explored later in this chapter, but for the current excerpt, it suffices to say that the Aspect gives temporal information about the Index rather than ascribing it with a quality or to a category. When spatio-temporal information is involved in a clause, it is usually accompanied with a non-mandatory status (i.e. whereas relational Processes must have an Index and Aspect, Circumstances can be included or omitted without impacting the validity of the realized clause). However, in instances such as Excerpt 4.18, the Aspect conflates with the Circumstance, making it a necessary component in the clause structure.

The different kinds of relational Process can be summarized in the system networks shown in Figure 4.9. In brief, on selecting [relational] from possible Process types, an Index and an Aspect are introduced into the clause. A tripartite choice is then presented, depending on whether notions of being (i.e. [intensive]), having (i.e. [possessive]) or being at (i.e. [circumstantial]) are to be expressed. Selections of [possessive] are the only ones to require the realization of an overt Process in the clause, typically via signs such as HAVE. Selections of [circumstantial] are the only options that result in further possible choices and, as discussed later in the chapter, interact with the network of CIRCUMSTANCE (shown in an abridged manner in Figure 4.9).

Indeterminacy in behavioural and existential Processes

The final Process types to be considered are behavioural and existential, which require insight into the notion of indeterminacy of categorization. Although such indeterminacy can occur across all experiential Process types (Gwilliams and

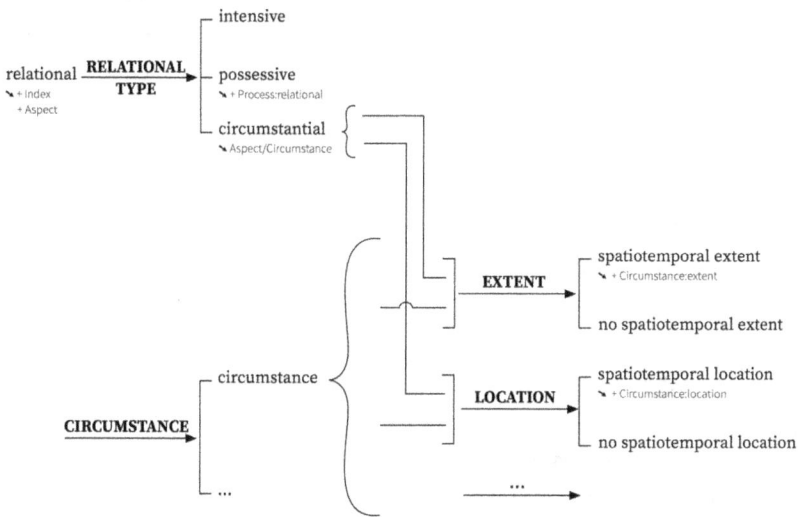

Figure 4.9 BSL systems for relational Process types.

Fontaine, 2015), this is typologically prominent for behavioural and existential Processes (Matthiessen, 2004b).

Behavioural Processes are understood as those elements of experience that incorporate 'physiological and psychological behaviour, like breathing, coughing, smiling, dreaming and staring' (Halliday and Matthiessen, 2014, p. 301). Whereas the material, mental, verbal and relational Processes discussed so far appear to have specific and recurrent patterns of functional composition in BSL clauses, behavioural Processes tend to blur with other Process types, both semantically and in terms of these realization patterns. An example of this indeterminacy is shown in Excerpt 4.19:

[4.19]

I	**Manual**	BEFORE	PT:PRO1SG	USUAL	CA:DAYDREAM
	Experiential	Circumstance	Participant	Circumstance	Participant | Process

In the past, I regularly daydreamed.

Broad experiential functions are presented in Excerpt 4.19 to show how this might be analysed from more than one perspective. Following Halliday and Matthiessen's (2014) abovementioned definition of behavioural Processes, the action of daydreaming could arguably fall into the realm of a psychological behaviour which may or may not call on conscious effort to perform. However, this could equally be analysed as a clause realizing a mental Process; the act of daydreaming is an internal experience, which is what mental Processes encompass from experiential perspectives. When observing the possible selections for mental Processes in Figure 4.7, this clause fits the selection of [mental: not-projecting: absent] (i.e. PT:PRO1SG is Senser, CA:DAYDREAM is Process:material and the two Circumstances are optional elements). Similar indeterminacy is noted in Rudge (2018), albeit between potential behavioural Processes and their interpretations as realizations of material Processes. As such, it remains tricky to identify a set of behavioural Processes that have distinct patterning in their realizations when compared to those found in other Process types. This is not to say that a behavioural Process distinction does not occur in BSL, but further investigation is required.

When considering existential Processes in BSL – those that indicate the existence of an element of experience – similar issues arise. These Processes have been observed in other languages through specific lexicogrammatical patterning. For instance, in English, the copula *to be* and its co-occurrence with the existential particle *there* – understood as 'neither a Participant nor a Circumstance' (Halliday and Matthiessen, 2014, p.308) – realize these existential Processes (e.g. *There is a tree*). Conversely, in Spanish, the verb *haber* can be used in an existential manner alongside the element of experience that is being referred to (e.g. *Hay un árbol;* see Lavid, Arús and Zamorano-Mansilla, 2010).

As noted previously, there is no specific verb sign or verbal group realization with regard to Processes of 'being'. Relatedly, there does not seem to be a verbal construction for 'existing' (or at least this is the case for what has been observed in the BSL datasets for this work and in other works, such as Rudge, 2018). Nonetheless, THERE is recognized as a fully lexical sign and has been glossed alongside EXIST in other resources (e.g. the BSL Signbank; Fenlon et al., 2014a), thereby suggesting a potential existential Process marker. However, as with behavioural Processes, difficulty arises when considering its distinction from other Process types, with realizations of circumstantial relational Processes forming the point of dispute in this case. Excerpt 4.20 provides insight as to why this difficulty occurs:

[4.20]

J	Spatio-kinetic		directed towards location in the signing space
	Manual	SHOP	THERE
	Experiential	Participant	x

As with Excerpt 4.19, broad experiential functions are ascribed in Excerpt 4.20: SHOP realizes a Participant, but THERE is ascribed with 'x' as a placeholder. If analysed as an existential particle, the translation may be *There is a shop*. However, THERE is produced with a movement in the signing space towards a specific point which, a few clauses later, the signer re-references using a locative pointing sign. Consequently, Excerpt 4.20 may instead be translated as something akin to *The shop is over there* wherein THERE provides information on the topographic location of SHOP. This alternative analysis therefore suggests a relational Process, with 'x' acting instead as a conflation of Aspect and Circumstance (see Excerpt 4.18 and Figure 4.9).

As with behavioural Processes, it remains tricky to find specific and stable points of disambiguation to confirm that existential Processes are seen in BSL. This is not to dismiss them from the discussion, as more in-depth analyses across further data may reveal the abovementioned patterns necessary to argue their place more confidently. Nonetheless, at this point, they remain too indeterminate to present as distinct systems.

Circumstances

The predominant focus of this chapter so far has been on the elements of Process and Participant. As alluded to at several points, however, the element of Circumstance also plays a part across the experiential metafunction, and thus needs to be considered. Circumstances are viewed as the more 'peripheral' elements of the clause: those that serve to augment the meaning being expressed in various manners, but that are not necessarily integral to the compositional validity of the clause. In other words, whereas a Process and its associated Participants are necessary to realize core experiential meanings, Circumstances are, for the most part, optional (the exception occurring with circumstantial relational Processes, as explained above). The areas of meaning expressed in this element include times, locations and the ways in which Processes are enacted by Participants.

Systemic functional descriptions of languages such as English demonstrate a variety of circumstantial sub-types, with Halliday and Matthiessen (2014) identifying no fewer than nine of them. According to the analyses performed across datasets for BSL, however, there appear to be four predominant sub-types of Circumstance. These are exemplified in Excerpts 4.21, 4.22 and 4.23, each drawn from the current dataset:

[4.21]

J	**Manual**	LAST-YEAR	FRIEND	PT:PRO3SG	EVERY-DAY	EXERCISE
	Experiential	Circ:location		Actor	Circ:extent	Process: material

Last year, (my) friend exercised every day.

[4.22]

S	**Spatio-kin.**					$3 \rightarrow 1$
	Manual	PT:PRO1SG	FRANCE	GO	DOG PT:PRO3SG	WITH
	Experiential	Actor	Scope	Pr:material	Circumstance: accompaniment	

I went to France with (my) dog.

[4.23]

J	**Non-manual**				furrowed brow; puffed cheeks
	Manual	IDEA	PT:PRO1SG	QUICK	CA:WRITE-EXTENSIVELY
	Experiential	Goal	Actor	Circ:manner	Actor | Pr:material | Circ:manner

I quickly scribbled down the idea.

In Excerpt 4.21, two signs are attributed as Circumstance: LAST-YEAR as location and EVERY-DAY as extent. Both offer temporal information adding to the meaning, but these are not necessarily 'required' from an experiential perspective (i.e. Excerpt 4.21 without these two realizations of Circumstances would still be understood, although the specifics of when actions occurred would not be known). While both temporal in nature, LAST-YEAR and EVERY-DAY are ascribed as location and extent respectively because the former indicates a particular point in time and the latter is concerned with the frequency of an action or event. Note, too, that while both instances in Excerpt 4.21 represent an aspect of time, these Circumstances may also concern location (e.g. locations and distances); hence, these are more adequately referred to as Circumstances that implicate spatiotemporal meanings.[7]

In Excerpt 4.22, a Circumstance of accompaniment is realized. In this case, the construction of the clause allows for the identification of the material Process, the Actor and the Scope,[8] which is then terminated with the addition of what seems to be a further Participant (as DOG PT:PRO3SG is a nominal group). However, the use of WITH alongside the noted movement in the signing space is what permits this preceding nominal group to be experientially categorized as the realization of an accompaniment. If WITH had been omitted, then DOG PT:PRO3SG would have had to be classed as a third Participant in the clause, although this would then require modification to material Process systems (see Figure 4.6) as there is no benefaction occurring and DOG PT:PRO3SG could not be functionally classed in this case as a Recipient.

In Excerpt 4.23, Circumstances of manner are realized in two ways. Initially, the signer uses the fully lexical sign QUICK to indicate how the Actor performed the Process of writing. Then, in following sequence of constructed action, the signer brings attention to the manner of the Process again via a quicker than usual movement accompanied by non-manual elements providing a sense of speed and/or effortfulness. Excerpt 4.23, therefore, demonstrates how Circumstantial information can be realized through manual means alone, and through combinations of manual, non-manual and spatio-kinetic elements.

To summarize, the four Circumstantial choices for BSL are as follows: EXTENT concerns spatiotemporal lengths and frequencies; LOCATION concerns specific times or places; MANNER concerns how a Process is performed; and ACCOMPANIMENT concerns additional, non-essential parties who do not otherwise realize functional Participants of the clause under analysis. Altogether, these may be combined into the broader system of CIRCUMSTANCE shown in Figure 4.10. This system operates simultaneously with PROCESS TYPE

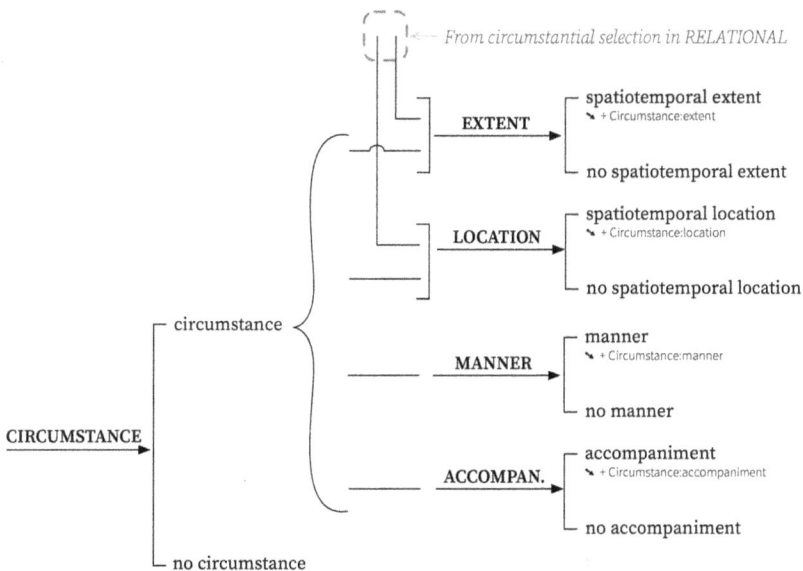

Figure 4.10 BSL system of CIRCUMSTANCE.

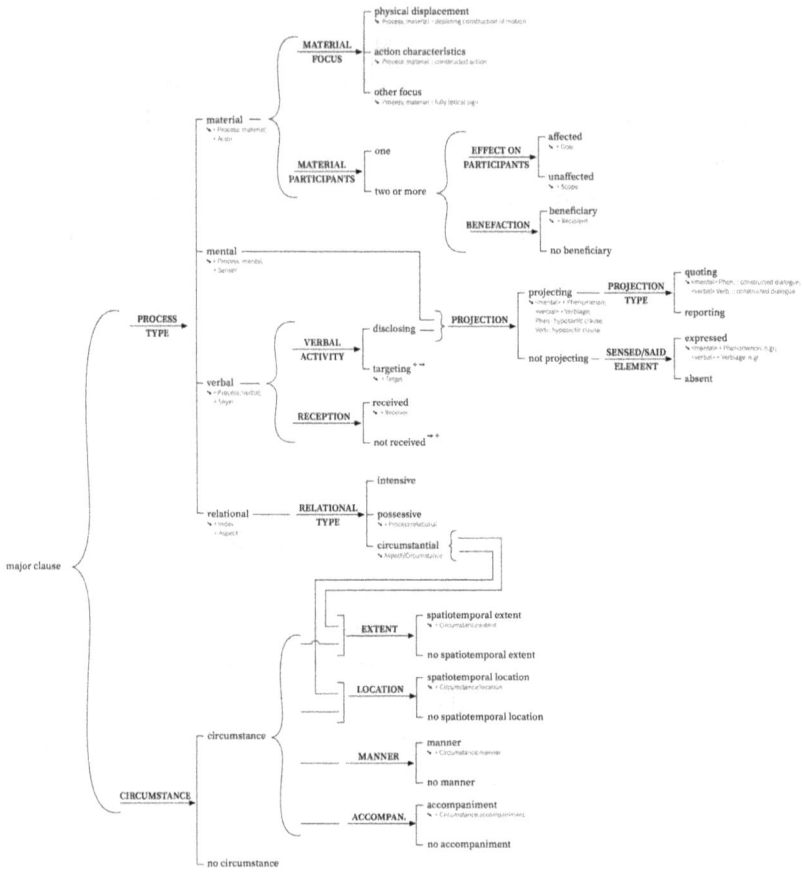

Figure 4.11 The experiential systems of BSL.

(see Figure 4.11) and has residual links to the RELATIONAL system seen in Figure 4.9. CIRCUMSTANCE allows for an initial binary choice of whether one or more Circumstances are to be included or none at all. If the former choice is selected, subsequent systems display choices in a way that a combination of any of the four types of Circumstance is possible (e.g. [spatiotemporal extent] and [manner] alongside [no spatiotemporal location] and [no accompaniment]).

The experiential networks of BSL

The experiential system networks from a transitive perspective are schematized in Figure 4.11. With the major clause as the entry condition, the system immediately splits into the simultaneous systems of PROCESS TYPE and

CIRCUMSTANCE, which then split into the more delicate systems and choices discussed in this chapter.

An extended experiential analysis can now be performed on a longer excerpt of BSL text from the dataset used for this chapter. In the following discourse, a BSL user is explaining a recent event wherein they met with a friend to go to a sporting goods shop (for further context: immediately prior to this excerpt, the signer explains that their old tennis racket was due to be replaced but that they were not sure of what to look for, hence asking their more experienced friend to assist).

[4.24]

i

Manual	RECENT	FRIEND	PT:PRO3SG	MEET
Experiential	Circ:location		Scope	Actor | Pr:material

I recently met a friend.

ii

Manual	BOTH	SPORT	SHOP	GO
Experiential	Actor		Scope	Pr:material

We both went to a sports shop

iii

Manual	WHY	PT:PRO1SG	NEW	TENNIS	RACKET	WANT
Experiential		Senser		Phenomenon		Pr:mental

because I wanted a new tennis racket.

iv

Manual	BOTH	WALK	ABOUT	TWENTY	MINUTE
Experiential	Actor	Pr:material	Circumstance:extent		

We walked for about 20 minutes.

v

Manual	DC:TWO-PEOPLE-WALKING
Experiential	Actor | Pr:material

We walked (to the shop)

vi

Spatio-kinetic	abrupt halt of manual motion path
Non-manual	widened eye aperture; slight backwards 'head jolt'
Manual	DC:TWO-PEOPLE-STOP-SUDDENLY
Experiential	Actor | Pr:material | Circumstance:manner

(but then) we both stopped in our tracks.

vii	**Manual**	PT:PRO1SG	SHOCK
	Experiential	Index	Aspect
		I (was) shocked	

viii	**Non-manual**				wide eye aperture; cheeks puffed
	Manual	WHY	SHOP	PT:PRO3SG	VERY-BIG
	Experiential		Index		Aspect
		because the shop was huge!			

ix	**Manual**	BEFORE	PT:PRO1SG	THINK
	Experiential	Circumstance:location	Senser	Process:mental
		I previously thought		

x	**Manual**	PT:PRO3SG	FEW	THINGS	HAVE
	Experiential	Index	Aspect		Process:relational
		[Phenomenon projected from previous clause]			
		that it (would) have some items			

xi	**Manual**	BUT	LOTS	HAVE
	Experiential		Aspect	Process:relational
		but (it) had loads (of things).		

Excerpt 4.24 demonstrates an array of Process types, Participants and Circumstances. While not covering all possible selections from the system networks shown in Figure 4.11, they do exemplify typical constructions and some points of interest. (i) and (ii), for example, realize material Processes, with the Actor in (i) realized simultaneously with the Process MEET. (iii) exemplifies the realization of a non-projecting mental Process, and although the Phenomenon refers to a physical object (i.e. NEW TENNIS RACKET), the Process WANT nonetheless expresses a desire rather than a physical action.

(v) and (vi) present further levels of realizational and analytical complexity. (v) picks up on information stated in the preceding clause (i.e. the location towards which the two Participants were moving) and instead focuses on the physical path movement from one location to another, hence being realized as a depicting construction incorporating both the Actor and the material Process (not dissimilar from that seen in Figure 4.3). However, (vi) suggests an abrupt stop to the motion within the same depicting construction, accompanied by relevant non-manual features to enhance the fact that the motion ended deliberately. As such, the depicting construction in (vi) is understood to realize the Actor, the material Process *and* Circumstantial manner.

From (vii) onwards (except for (ix)), various relational constructions are presented. (vii) and (viii) select for [relational: intensive], resulting in the absence of a Process sign, whereas (x) and (xi) select for [relational: possessive], with the relational Process realized by HAVE. (ix) shows a second example of a mental Process, but unlike (iii), [projecting] is selected. This projection is represented in (x) which contains two experiential glosses: one as the projected Phenomenon of the previous clause and the other as the possessive relational Process occurring within (x) itself.

Summary

This chapter has demonstrated that when experience is understood from a transitive perspective, patterns and distinctions within the lexicogrammar of BSL occur. Languages provide us with a vehicle through which experiences – whether ours or another's; whether recent, centuries ago or thousands of years in the future – can be expressed. Although the domains of experience suggested in this chapter are wide-ranging, it is nonetheless possible to see order within this potentially chaotic situation by breaking down 'phenomena' into broad components at the level of discourse semantics, and then exploring realizational correlates and patterns in the lexicogrammatical stratum. This was performed here using the systems of PROCESS TYPE and CIRCUMSTANCE.

The experiential system networks developed for BSL are relatively stable. However, as discussed at various points in this chapter, there are still several experiential pathways yet to be investigated in further detail. This includes, for instance, a closer look at the ergative model of experience in BSL, further explorations of lexicogrammatical patterning for behavioural and existential Processes, and opportunities to expand on the nascent networks presented in the system of CIRCUMSTANCE. These and other areas of exploration are summarized in Chapter 7 for ease of reference.

Exploring the Textual Metafunction

This work has so far explored BSL regarding the negotiation of meaning between language users (i.e. interpersonal matters) and the representation of experience (i.e. ideational/experiential matters). As robust and informative as these may be in understanding how BSL is used across communicative contexts, there remains one crucial aspect that needs to be addressed: the way in which interpersonal and ideational/experiential meanings can be expressed in a cohesive manner over time. BSL is not produced in a haphazard manner, but opportunities to linguistically negotiate and ideate require assistance from a third resource to ensure that there is cohesion in what is being signed, particularly in relation to 'what went before' and 'what is to come'. This is the domain of the textual metafunction, which enables and ties together interpersonal and ideational/experiential meaning.

This chapter explores the textual metafunction using a broadly similar structure to the previous two chapters. To begin, the textual metafunction is introduced from a trinocular perspective, briefly exploring the contextual variable of mode and selected associated discourse semantic systems. It then moves on to a more detailed treatment of the lexicogrammatical stratum to understand how textual meaning is realized, using examples from a dataset of recorded BSL interactions. As will be ascertained quite quickly in this chapter, the textual metafunction is expansive in its scope and complex when considering the potential for interactions with other metafunctions. For the sake of simplicity and for ease of comparison with content in Chapters 3 and 4, this chapter focuses on clause-level concerns. From a textual perspective, this predominantly concerns the functional components of Theme and Rheme, although other functions including Given and New are also discussed. Through analysis and description of excerpts from the dataset, the systems of MULTIPLE THEME, THEME ELLIPSIS and CLAUSE FOCUS are presented and exemplified, prior to being compiled into a larger textual network. Finally, a textual analysis of an extended excerpt is offered to demonstrate how choices from these systems are made in discourse.

Whereas the nature of the interpersonal metafunction was viewed as prosodic, and that of the experiential metafunction was viewed as componential or particulate, the textual metafunction is instead understood to be periodic. To use a common analogy found across systemic functional literature, textual concerns are those that appear to act in a wave-like manner, with an ebb and flow throughout a text. These waves are visible at various magnifications ranging from individual clauses through to full interactions, but as alluded to above, the focus of this chapter will remain lexicogrammatically at clause rank. In doing so, this chapter provides a necessary and sufficiently robust platform from which a wealth of further textual concerns in BSL can be successfully investigated in the future. For ease of reference, these further textual points of interest are collated in Chapter 7.

Making sense and making waves

A text's cohesive flow relies on several lexicogrammatical features, but it is nonetheless influenced and shaped by the extra-textual environment in which it occurs. The contextual variable primarily associated with the textual metafunction (i.e. when viewed 'from above') is mode, concerning aspects such as a text's manner of delivery and its overall communicative function or purpose. This includes, amongst other factors, the medium through which the communication occurs; the extent to which the communication is truly spontaneous or has been previously planned; whether the communication is monologic or dialogic; the intended function of the communication (i.e. its rhetorical mode, such as instructing, narrating or persuading); and how the text is oriented regarding ideational/informative or interpersonal/affective concerns. Put another way, this contextual component is 'concerned with the role played by language in the context in which it operates' (Matthiessen, Teruya and Lam, 2010, p.144) or 'the role language is playing in realising social action' (Martin, 1992, p.508). Whereas tenor (Chapter 3) and field (Chapter 4) are concerned with aspects of context that are often identifiable as 'distinct' from a given text (i.e. relations between communicative parties and action/experience, respectively), mode and its various components can instead be understood as expressed *through* a given text.

Moving from context and into the topmost linguistic stratum of discourse semantics (i.e. when viewed 'from roundabout'), it is perhaps understandable that there is a wealth of systems found here, given the various aspects of mode noted above. To both provide background into this wide-ranging area and to shift the focus onto more clause-level concerns, a brief survey of some systems found at this stratum follows.

The discourse semantic systems of IDENTIFICATION and TRACKING (see Martin and Rose, 2007) relate to elements of meaning most closely associated with experiential Participants, thereby typically having an assumed closer association to ranks below that of the clause, such as group and word. In brief, a text's cohesion (or its 'texture'; Halliday and Hasan, 1976) requires Participants involved within the text to be referenced and re-referenced in a logical, coherent manner. To achieve this, two systems can be called on: IDENTIFICATION, concerning the introduction of Participants in a text and how they are referred to (e.g. using a full name vs a generalized pronoun) and TRACKING, concerning the recoverability of identified Participants and in which 'direction' the text points to obtain this information, such as co-textually or contextually (i.e. phoricity; see Chapter 5 of Martin and Rose, 2007). Successful identification and tracking are necessary to achieve texture because, for instance, if someone were recounting an extended event involving multiple Participants, there would need to be an understandable flow of who did what, and at which points. Being unable to reference or track would likely lead to unintelligibility.

The strong experiential/ideational slant to IDENTIFICATION and TRACKING suggests that these textual systems more closely enable aspects of experience and ideation (i.e. of Participants) than they do of interpersonal negotiation. However, contextual influences within the more interpersonal domain of tenor may influence selections available in these systems. For example, an aspect of mode includes the rhetorical function of a text, such as recounting. Yet, the way in which recounting occurs also depends on various interpersonal factors between the person recounting and their audience. Discourse of a relationship gone awry when recounted to a group of close friends (*I couldn't believe what that idiot did*), compared to the same discourse being recounted to a family law solicitor (*I couldn't believe what Mr Smith did*), may require variations in the resultant lexicogrammatical realizations of choices in IDENTIFICATION and TRACKING. This short exposition serves as a twofold reminder. Firstly, while metafunctions have been presented in this book as individual concerns, there is significant interaction between them in any given stretch of discourse (explored in further detail in Chapter 6). Secondly, and relatedly, the textual metafunction may facilitate and interact more with either ideational or interpersonal aspects of meaning, but in doing so, it does not 'abandon' the other metafunction.

Other than identifying and tracking elements across a text, it is also necessary to consider how a text can be used to manage the flow of information being produced. As well as being cohesive, a text needs to carry information in such a way that its development makes sense. For instance, had Chapter 3 of this book opened with an in-depth comparison of two interpersonal systems, only to be followed five pages later by an introduction for the chapter, the flow of information would be stilted because the introduction prepares the reader for what is to come in the remainder of the text. This information flow involves interaction between the levels of discourse structure (e.g. *Introduction, Section A, Section B* and so on, until reaching the *Conclusion*) and, as a logical consequence, between lexicogrammatical levels: paragraphs allow for information flow and change within and between themselves, as do larger sentences, all the way to the level of individual clauses.

This flow of information is referred to by Martin and Rose (2007) as PERIODICITY, which is theorized at various levels at which this flow occurs. They note this effect is pulse-like or, to use a metaphor used across systemic functional literature, wave-like:[1]

> Discourse creates expectations by flagging forward and consolidates them by summarizing back. These expectations are presented as crests of information, and the meanings fulfilling these expectations can be seen as relative diminuendos, from the point of view of information flow. The term *periodicity* is used to capture the regularity of information flow: the tendency for crests to form a regular pattern, and for the hierarchy of waves to form a predictable rhythm.
>
> (Martin and Rose, 2007, p.189)

Wave-like prominence at clause level can be understood from intersecting perspectives. In general, an assumption is made that there will be two contrasting parts of a clause with regard to information flow: one part will form the 'peak' of the information wave and the other the 'trough'. Overall, there are three dichotomous pairs of clause-level functional elements that resonate with textual concerns: Theme and Rheme; Given and New; and Topic and Comment.

Much of the current thinking around clause-level textual concerns is rooted within the work of the Prague School (e.g. Mathesius, 1939) and ideas of information structure. These ideas have been subject to (re)interpretation and expansion from several perspectives, which have led to a significant amount of discrepancy in the way that original terms have been employed and adapted. Space does not permit a full exploration of the intricacies (although works such as LaPolla, 2020 offer an excellent overview) but a surface-level overview is presented here to introduce the matters at hand.

A predominant textual 'split' within a clause can be seen between the functional Theme and Rheme, with the former being 'the point of departure of the clause as *message*' (Matthiessen, Teruya and Lam, 2010, p.222; emphasis added). LaPolla (2020) offers an extended interpretation of Theme (via Firbas, 1987) as 'the item with the lowest degree of communicative dynamism in the clause' (LaPolla, 2020, p.162) and that which 'provides the foundation [...] for the information provided in the rest of the clause' (ibid.). From typological perspectives, Matthiessen (2004b) notes that 'Theme tends to be realised by initial position in the clause' (p.642) but likewise identifies that this is not a universal (e.g. Japanese; see Teruya, 2007). Rheme, consequently, is the remainder of the clause not ascribed to Theme. In English, for instance, the Theme is generally understood to occur initially (i.e. providing the local context of the clause) and the Rheme follows. The transition point between the two generally conflates with the split between the interpersonal Subject and Finite, or the point at which an experiential Process is introduced (see Halliday and Matthiessen, 2014), as suggested in Excerpts 5.1 and 5.2:

[5.1]

English	The new academic year	had been eagerly anticipated.
Textual	Theme	Rheme

[5.2]

English	It	crept up on us.
Textual	Theme	Rheme

The above excerpts provide simplistic instances of Theme-Rheme distinctions in English, wherein Theme also conflates with the Subject and the first experiential Participant, whether realized as a single pronoun (Excerpt 5.2), or as an extended nominal group (Excerpt 5.1). While such textual distinctions are viewed overall as unproblematic, other works do offer alternative perspectives. Forey and Sampson (2017), for instance, suggest a far more fluid ascription of Theme, to the extent that 'what is analysed as Theme is dependent on the aim and purpose of the analysis' (p.143).

Halliday (1967) expanded on Prague School perspectives of Theme and Rheme, and presented the simultaneous textual functions of Given and New. Whereas the former functional pair offers insight into the structure and the clause-level contextualization of information, the latter pair of functions concern elements of focus and information novelty. In brief, Halliday refers to New parts of a clause as focal points, with New used 'not in the sense that is cannot have been previously mentioned [...], but in the sense that the speaker presents it as not being recoverable from the preceding discourse' (p.204). The remainder of the clause is then ascribed as Given. Furthermore, similar to discussions regarding the interpersonal metafunction (see Chapter 3), phonological elements such as tonic prominence have also been argued for in the identification of New parts of a clause (see Halliday and Greaves, 2008; Halliday and Matthiessen, 2014; and O'Grady, 2017 for perspectives on English).

In Excerpts 5.1 and 5.2 above, if the textual tier were expanded to include Given and New, we would expect conflation with Theme and Rheme respectively: the point of departure for the clause that sets the local context (Theme) would generally link with information that is retrievable from content or co-text (Given), with the remaining information (Rheme) being less predictable (New). However, at this point, it is important to (re-)establish that Theme-Rheme and Given-New operate as two independent functional dyads. To exemplify this, Excerpt 5.3a is extracted from an example given by Halliday and Greaves (2008) wherein a spoken narrative is analysed. The authors note that *I was* realizes the textually Given function:

[5.3a]

English	I was	apprenticed engineer
Textual	Given	New

The boundaries of these textual functions can shift depending on factors such as the part of the clause that the language user wishes to focus on or given prominence to, again, using phonological resources to assist with this. In other words, intonational prominence can 'shift' the Given-New boundary to something more marked, and when combining Theme and Rheme with what is shown in Excerpt 5.3a, it is possible to demonstrate an offset between the two, as shown in Excerpt 5.3b:

[5.3b]

English	I	was	apprenticed engineer
Textual	Theme		Rheme
		Given	New

These (mis)matches in functions will be developed in more detail in the following section when considering the textual grammar of BSL. Prior to this, the final pairing noted above – Topic and Comment – requires elaboration. In LaPolla's (2020) exploration of the distinction between the pairings noted so far, he argues for a point of distinction 'between the Theme, defined as the speaker's starting point, and the Topic, what the clause is about' (p.174), while also noting that Topic 'is independent of, though often overlaps with, both "given" and "point of departure" (Theme)' (p.178). While in practice it can be tricky to tease out the exact distinctions between Theme, Given and Topic from a cross-linguistic perspective, it is nonetheless interesting that a variety of works concerning constituent orders in sign languages – disregarding those focusing on more formal perspectives (e.g. Sandler and Lillo-Martin, 2006) – often note a topic-comment constituent order (e.g. Jantunen, 2007; Sutton-Spence and Woll, 1999; cf. Johnston, 2019, who investigates Auslan constituent order from Role and Reference Grammar (RRG) perspectives). However, due to few definitions of these terms being offered within such works, it is not completely clear if this distinction is used in the way proposed by Prague School linguists (i.e. 'topic-focus articulation'; see Mathesius, 1939, and Firbas, 1987) or if it is used as a method to identify a broad point of distinction between 'what comes first' and 'what can be communicated about what comes first'. The perspectives presented in the following section do not aim to discredit these latter views. Instead, this work intends to be complementary to the findings of studies across the range of both sign linguistics and systemic functionalism, and attempts to expand on the complexities of textual organization in BSL while developing this understanding beyond current perspectives.

Towards a textual grammar of BSL

The clause-level functions of Theme and Rheme form the main area of focus in this exploration of the textual metafunction in BSL, although additional functions such as Given and New will be identified where relevant. To investigate how text and texture develop in BSL, a somewhat experimental recording setup was used in terms of data collection. Pairs of BSL users who knew one another were invited to sit facing one another, but only one of the two participants was able to see a projector screen. The participant facing the screen was asked to watch, and then later recount in BSL, a small excerpt from an episode of the cartoon *Mr Bean: The Animated Series* (based on the original 1990s comedy series starring Rowan Atkinson).[2] This series was chosen as it rarely has fundamental spoken dialogue, and for the most part, the animations are elaborate enough for events to be communicated through static images, character actions and any consequences of these actions. Each episode runs for approximately ten minutes, but as this was not intended as a test of memory, the excerpts were played in segments of approximately ninety seconds in which characters performed a series of actions that could be recounted in a specific sequence (e.g. Mr Bean parking in a 'parent and child only' parking space, being chastised by a stranger for doing so, brushing off these concerns, covertly wrapping a stuffed toy in fabric and finally moving past the stranger pretending he had a child).

While more experimental in its nature that the data collection methods used in Chapters 3 and 4, this setup was otherwise intended to be as informal as possible: participants knew each other well; they were permitted to communicate about other topics in-between instances of recounting; and there was no obligation to provide a perfect recitation of the story. However, to enable as much textual cohesion as possible during the recounting phase, the 'receptive' participant in the pair was asked not to interrupt or request clarification until after the recounting was complete (nonetheless permitting backchanneling and reactions such as humour or shock). This resulted in a rich dataset permitting an exploration of textual, logogenetic patterning, as exemplified and explained below.

Theme, Rheme and MULTIPLE THEME

Following the interpretations of Theme and Rheme as discussed earlier in this chapter (i.e. wherein Theme represents the 'local context' of the clause), it is possible to demonstrate broad functional distinctions at clause level in BSL from textual perspectives. Excerpts 5.4 and 5.5 provide our first examples of this:

[5.4]

C	Non-manual	brow raise	squinted eyes; brow furrow
	Manual	PT:PRO3SG	CA:PEER-THROUGH-WINDOW
	Textual	Theme	Rheme

He peered through the window.

[5.5]

B	Non-manual	brow raise		
	Manual	CAR	PT:POSS3SG	GREEN
	Textual	Theme		Rheme

His car (was) green.

In Excerpt 5.4, the signer begins the clause by identifying an experiential Participant realized through one pronominal pointing sign, indicating a referent that was designated earlier in the dialogue. C then uses constructed action to mimetically embody the Process of the identified Participant. Similarly, in Excerpt 5.5, a Participant is realized clause-initially – albeit slightly more complex than Excerpt 5.4 with two manual signs rather than one – followed by a final sign ascribing a value or distinction to the previously signed information (i.e. a [relational: intensive] selection in the system of PROCESS TYPE; see Chapter 4).

As a general observation from the wider dataset, Theme appears to occur clause-initially in BSL with Rheme following, suggesting that these textual functions are realized by position within the clause. However, Excerpts 5.4 and 5.5 above also include the glossing of non-manual elements, particularly the position of the signer's eyebrows. In the exploration of the interpersonal grammar of BSL in Chapter 3, eyebrow position (and its relationship to intonation and the plane of expression) was indicated to be a core point of distinction between various choices in MOOD which tend to occur clause-finally. For instance, a clause realized with the same manual components but with different eyebrow heights can result in a distinction between [declarative] and [interrogative] feature selections in MOOD. In textual terms, the eyebrows appear to play a similar role from the perspective of visual intonation, playing a part in the realization of Theme as well as marking the transition point into Rheme. Changes in other non-manual features may also occur at this transition point (e.g. slumping the shoulders, squinting the eyes and so on) although these are not as frequent as changes in eyebrow height. Different combinations of these features may be due to individual signer preference or as preparation for what is to be signed immediately after. Such possibilities begin to move beyond the scope of the current chapter, but it is nonetheless a worthwhile area for future investigation.

It would be an oversimplification to say that clauses like those presented in Excerpts 5.4 and 5.5 represent the breadth of possibilities regarding textual organization in BSL. In fact, the textual metafunction has various systems at the lexicogrammatical stratum with variations and additions to the Theme and Rheme structure noted in the previous excerpts. The first of these variations concerns clause-initial elements that are found within the scope of the broader Theme, and that accompany what shall now be more specifically labelled as topical Theme (i.e. the part of the Theme most closely aligned with experiential functions). An example is provided in Excerpt 5.6:

[5.6]

L	Non-manual	brow raise					
	Manual	MAYBE	PT:PRO3SG	THING	PT:LOC	SEE	CAN
	Textual	Theme:int.	Theme:topical	Rheme			
		Maybe he can see that thing					

L	Non-manual	brow raise			headshake
	Manual	BUT	TRUE	PT:LOC	NOTHING
	Textual	Theme:text.	Theme:int.	Theme:top.	Rheme
		but, really, it's not there.			

Excerpt 5.6 displays two clauses produced in succession, in which an overall split can be seen between textual functions (with non-manual elements again aligning at points of transition between these). However, Theme now appears more nuanced in its composition, such that multiple Themes are identified – the topical Theme (which are also those elements that were ascribed as Theme in Excerpts 5.4 and 5.5), the interpersonal Theme and the textual Theme.

An interpersonal Theme occurs when a manual or non-manual construal of judgement, stance or point of view is provided prior to the topical Theme in the clause. It is associated with interpersonal meanings such as those discussed in Chapter 3 because it involves interactive, 'negotiable' elements between language users. However, interpersonal Theme in BSL typically realizes meanings from the discourse semantic system of APPRAISAL than of SPEECH FUNCTION (i.e. emotional, evaluative and attitudinal elements of language; see Martin and White, 2005). In Excerpt 5.6, two interpersonal Themes are present, realized manually as MAYBE and TRUE. Both express aspects of the signer's engagement with the propositions at hand, the former suggesting the possibility of the Participant's ability to see an object and the latter establishing the contrasting truth of the situation.

Textual Theme operates in more of an organizational manner, assisting the connection and juxtaposition of multiple clauses such that the arrangement of the information from one clause to another makes sense (i.e. resonating with the textual metafunction; see Matthiessen, 1995 and Matthiessen, Teruya and Lam, 2010). In Excerpt 5.6, one instance of textual Theme is realized via BUT. This functions in a disjunctive manner and permits the apposition of the statement expressed in first clause with that of the second: 'this was perceived' versus 'this was the reality'.

The occurrence of multiple Themes is frequent in longer stretches of BSL discourse, such as those analysed in this chapter. Overall, interpersonal Theme

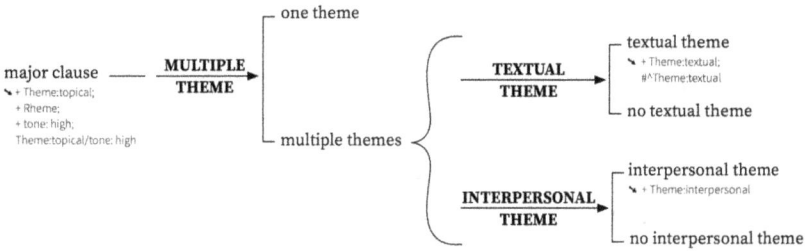

Figure 5.1 BSL system of MULTIPLE THEME.

reflects aspects such as the veracity claimed by the signer in recounting a story, and textual Theme permits the logical sequencing and linkage of information in previous clauses with information in forthcoming clauses. There are also patterns with regard to the sequencing and other relations between these elements. Firstly, in all clauses, a topical Theme is overtly realized (or at least easily recoverable, as will be discussed shortly), whereas the interpersonal and textual Themes are optional. Secondly, the topical Theme coincides with the use of non-manual components realizing a 'high' intonational tone (i.e. through the predominant use of raised eyebrows; see Chapter 3 for further argumentation on visual prosody in the interpersonal metafunction), with changes in non-manual elements generally signalling the transition point where Theme ends and Rheme begins. Finally, when all three types of functional Theme are present, they are ordered Theme:textual^Theme:interpersonal^Theme:topical. These findings are expressed in the system of MULTIPLE THEME in Figure 5.1.

THEME ELLIPSIS

As suggested above, the topical Theme is a core textual function of the clause in BSL, but its lexicogrammatical realization can vary to the extent that, in certain cases, it may have a 'null' realization (i.e. it can be ellipted). Excerpt 5.7 offers an extended example of this in action:

[5.7]

T	Spatio-kinetic			slight lean right	
	Non-manual	brow raise			
	Manual	WOMAN	PT:PRO3SG	HOME	LEAVE
	Textual	Theme:topical		Rheme	
		The woman left her house,			

T	**Spatio-kinetic**	slight lean left	
	Manual	WALK++	
	Textual	Rheme	
		(she) walked for some time,	
T	**Non-manual**	cheek puff	
	Manual	AT-LAST	ARRIVE
	Textual	Theme:interpersonal	Rheme
		(and) finally (she) arrived.	

The sequence of experiential Processes recounted in Excerpt 5.7 – leaving, walking and then arriving – was enacted by the Participant identified in the first clause, which at that point realized the topical Theme. No other Participant was realized across the following clauses, thereby reducing the ambiguity of 'who did what' in the sequence. As a result, the topical Theme is not overtly realized (e.g. as PT:PRO3SG, WOMAN and so on) in the second and third clauses of Excerpt 5.7, but it is nonetheless recoverable from the preceding co-text (i.e. it may be understood as Given rather than New). Put another way, the local context of the first clause is set out by the signer, and it then 'scopes' in such a way that its repetition, at least in this instance, may be viewed as redundant. This effect is likewise noted in work approaching sign language description from more formal perspectives, noting that 'topic-drop' can occur when 'the topic of a sentence can be deleted under identity with a topic in the preceding sentence(s)' (Pfau and Bos, 2016, p.142).

Other aspects of Excerpt 5.7 are worth noting, too. For example, between the first and second clauses, the signer uses an alternating body lean. This is likely to be related to logico-semantic concerns and elements of taxis (i.e. implicating the logical metafunction) where the change in the body lean may signal a paratactic expansion (see Halliday and Matthiessen, 1999). In addition, the third clause of Excerpt 5.7 still realizes the interpersonal Theme as FINALLY while the topical Theme remains ellipted. It would also be possible for a textual Theme to have been included in this clause prior to the interpersonal Theme (e.g. BUT) and for the topical Theme to have remained ellipted. As such, it can be suggested that the system of MULTIPLE THEME as presented in Figure 5.1 and the effect of ellipsis occurring here form two separate, but nonetheless related, systems.

As suggested in Chapter 3, topical Theme ellipsis may also occur when moves switch between signers. To highlight this effect, Excerpt 3.6 is repeated below as Excerpt 5.8, now with textual analysis:

[5.8]

L	Non-manual	brow raise	
	Manual	PT:PRO3SG	HEARING
	Textual	Theme:topical	Rheme

(Is) she a hearing person?

S	Non-manual	head nod
	Manual	HEARING
	Textual	Rheme

(She is) a hearing person.

Like earlier excerpts, the topical Theme in the second clause of Excerpt 5.9 is ellipted as it can be easily retrieved from the immediate co-text. It would have also been permissible for S to have realized the topical Theme by using a sign such as PT:PRO3SG, but in this flow of discourse between two people, it was ellipted.

There is a difficulty encountered with topical Theme ellipsis, however, with regard to its variability. From the BSL data analysed for this chapter, and across data collected for this work and beyond, identifying an exact pattern of when ellipsis occurs remains tricky to identify. Examples such as those in Excerpts 5.7 and 5.8 are useful starting points, but it is also possible for instances like those in Excerpt 5.9 to occur:

[5.9]

L	Non-manual	brow raise		head nod
	Manual	PT:PRO3SG	CHAIR	SIT
	Textual	Theme:topical	Rheme	

He sat on a chair

L	Non-manual	brow raise		
	Manual	NEXT	PT:PRO3SG	READ
	Textual	Theme:textual	Theme:topical	Rheme

then he read.

Given the ellipsis of topical Theme in Excerpts 5.7 and 5.8, it would have been expected that the topical Theme in the second clause of Excerpt 5.9 would have also been ellipted as the information of 'who did what' is still recoverable from

theme present

major clause ———— **THEME
ELLIPSIS**
↘ + Theme:topical;
 + Rheme;
 + tone: high;
 Theme:topical/tone: high

theme ellipted
↘ Theme:topical: Ø

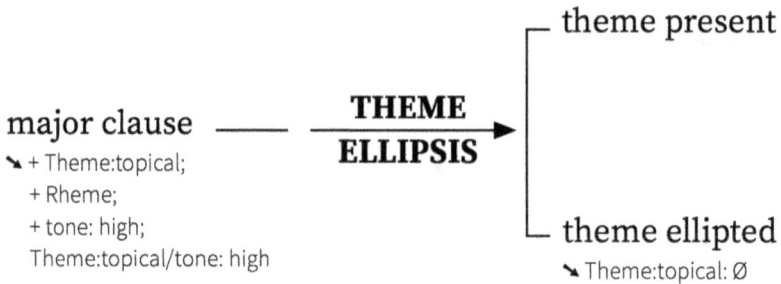

Figure 5.2 BSL system of THEME ELLIPSIS.

the preceding clause. The second realization of the topical Theme may therefore be used to provide an enhanced level of clarity or emphasis of identification (e.g. to make it obvious that it was a specific person from a selection of people who were previously identified in the dialogue). Nevertheless, in other cases, it may be down to a signer's idiolectal choices: some signers in the dataset seemed to ellipt topical Themes frequently, whereas others did so rarely.[3]

Despite this variation, the system of THEME ELLIPSIS can be proposed in an elementary state (see Figure 5.2), although further development of this system is encouraged. For the time being, it is schematized such that the optionality of whether to include or ellipt the topical Theme is not driven by any definite influences or requirements. Regardless, it does indicate that selections of [theme ellipted] result in a null ('Ø') realization of the topical Theme.

CLAUSE FOCUS

The final system presented in this chapter concerns Given and New, and how information prominence can be shifted within a clause, resonating strongly with the interpersonal metafunction. As a reminder, New in the textual sense is concerned with that which the language user wishes to focus as newsworthy, instead of referring to information that was 'not previously expressed'. The following also concerns interactions with the expression stratum (i.e. intonation and tonic prominence; see Fries, 2000; Halliday and Greaves, 2008; and Moore, 2016) and the broader system of VISUAL PROSODY introduced in Chapter 3.

An example of textually shifting clause focus is presented in Excerpt 5.10, wherein C uses combinations of manual and non-manual components to highlight interpersonal negative polarity:

[5.10]

C	Non-manual	brow raise			
	Manual	PT:PRO3SG	OBJECT	PT:DET	WANT
	Textual	Theme:topical		Rheme	

He wanted that object.

C	Non-manual	brow raise		headshake
	Manual	PT:PRO3SG	OBJECT	BUY
	Textual	Theme:topical	Rheme	

He did not buy (the) object.

As noted in the exploration of the interpersonal metafunction in Chapter 3, clauses with negative polarity are generally realized in BSL with the use of non-manual negation markers (i.e. a headshake towards or at the end of the clause). This is present in the second clause of Excerpt 5.10, indicated by *not* in the English gloss. There is, however, more complexity present in the second clause than just a headshake. Interpersonal MOOD also plays a marked part in this clause. The use of raised eyebrows throughout the clause up until the headshake would generally indicate an [interrogative: polar] selection (i.e. one that might be translated as *Did he buy (the) object?*). However, there is a change in the non-manual components where BUY acts as the locus of the change. Firstly, BUY is manually produced as the eyebrows remain raised. Then, as the internal movement component of BUY ends, the sign is held in the signing space (i.e. a post-stroke hold; see Kendon, 2004). During this hold, the eyebrows lower to a neutral position, and the headshakes. This is visualized in Figure 5.3.

Consequently, clauses such as those in Excerpt 5.10 suggest (at face value) that a question is being asked and that it is being answered immediately by the person asking (i.e. analogous to *Did he buy (the) object? No.*). These structures have been noted in other works as rhetorical or cleft constructions (see, e.g., Sutton-Spence and Woll, 1999), but the perspective taken in this work is different. Instead, these are instances of [declarative] realization wherein non-manual components visually realize intonation to highlight the interpersonal polarity in the development of the wider text. This has textual implications that require a more in-depth gloss to ensure accurate representation. This is offered in Excerpt 5.10b:

[5.10b]

C	Non-manual	brow raise		headshake
	Manual	PT:PRO3SG	OBJECT	BUY
	Textual	Theme:topical		Rheme
		Given		New

He did not by (the) object.

Excerpt 5.10b shows that the change in eyebrow height and the transition into a headshake form an important point regarding the realization of Given and New. Specifically, New begins when the headshake begins, thereby being introduced not by a manual sign alone, but by its *co-occurrence* with a clause-final, non-manual component as the manual sign is held. This is represented in Excerpt 5.10b by the vertical line in the non-manual and textual tiers splitting BUY (although the real-time realization may not be exactly halfway through the production of BUY itself).

In a similar vein to the examples shown above, a different kind of construction can also impact the typical Given-New conflation with topical Theme and Rheme. Two examples are shown in Excerpts 5.11 and 5.12, both employing the more elaborate analysis seen in Excerpt 5.10b:

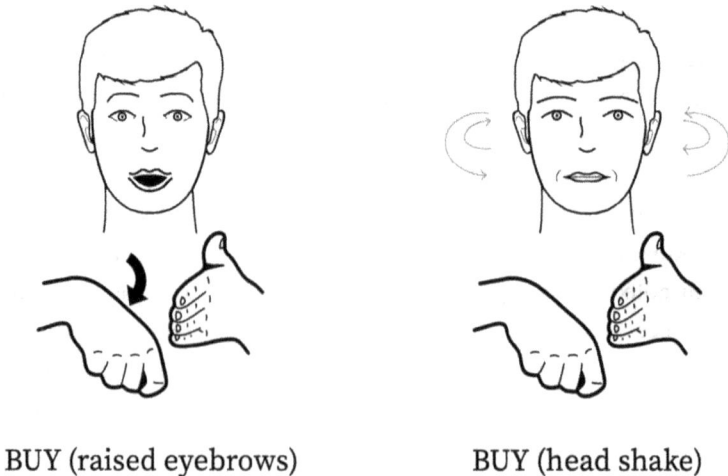

BUY (raised eyebrows)   BUY (head shake)

Figure 5.3 BUY accompanied with different non-manual components.

[5.11]

S					
Non-manual	brow raise			brow raise	head nod
Manual	PT:PRO3SG	FINISH		WHEN	YESTERDAY
Textual	Theme:topical			Rheme	
		Given			New

She finished yesterday.

[5.12]

C					
Non-manual		brow raise			
Manual	BEFORE	PT:PROS3SG	SEE	WHO	BROTHER
Textual	Theme:int.	Theme:topic.		Rheme	
		Given			New

Previously she had seen (her) brother.

In both excerpts, the focus – that which is New – is shifted to the end of the clause. For comparison, their 'non-focused' equivalent manual constructions could be YESTERDAY PT:PRO3SG FINISH and BEFORE PT:PRO3SG BROTHER SEE respectively.

Excerpts 5.11 and 5.12 have some similarities to Excerpts 5.10 and 5.10b above, but the focus now highlights experiential information rather than interpersonal information. Non-manual prosodic elements again appear to change at the Given-New boundary, with the key difference being the inclusion of an interpersonal Inquirer function, realized manually as a 'WH-' sign (i.e. WHEN, WHO, WHAT and so on) prior to the realization of New.

Two points require a little more unpacking. Firstly, as with the realization of elemental interrogatives (see Chapter 3), different realizations of the Inquirer function will result in different types of experiential information being focused. In Excerpt 5.11, WHEN is used to preface the realization of experientially temporal information, which in this case is a Circumstance of temporal location YESTERDAY. In Excerpt 5.12, WHO is used to preface the realization of a Participant in the clause, which in this case is BROTHER. Secondly, the height of the eyebrows that co-occur with the Inquirer forms a point of distinction. Rather than furrowing the brow to realize an [interrogative: elemental] selection (i.e. a move in which unknown information is requested), the brow is raised, signalling that the type of experiential information prefaced by the Inquirer is both known and about to be expressed by the signer themselves (i.e. information is being given, not demanded).

These textual structures therefore call on [interrogative] selections with modifications in both manual and non-manual visual prosody, impacting the

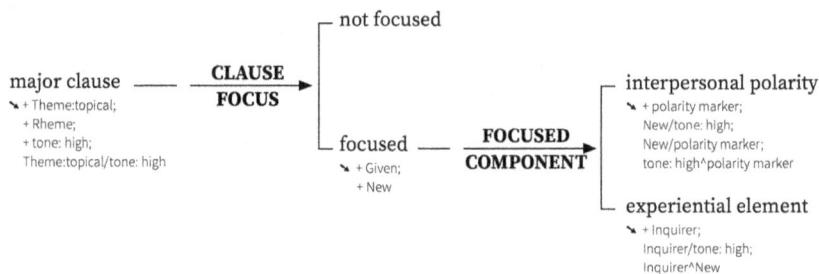

Figure 5.4 BSL system of CLAUSE FOCUS.[4]

alignment of Theme and Rheme with Given and New. Consequently, textual prominence can be attributed to either interpersonal polarity or experiential element (i.e. Participant, Process and Circumstance). To continue the analogy presented at the beginning of this chapter, these structures can shift the peak in the 'wave' of information and the focus of the clause, as schematized in the CLAUSE FOCUS system network presented in Figure 5.4.

The textual networks of BSL

Similar to Chapters 3 and 4, the textual system networks observed in this chapter can now be drawn together and presented collectively in Figure 5.5. The major clause once again acts as the entry point into the various primary textual systems, all acting as simultaneous choices and splitting into their more delicate systems as presented so far in this chapter.

To demonstrate these systems in use, an extended stretch of BSL is now analysed. In the following extended excerpt, taken from the same context as the examples given in this chapter, a BSL user is recapping part of an observed episode, wherein the protagonist has entered a shopping centre and is attempting to find a specific location. In this instance, a varied yet uninterrupted flow of discourse is offered, providing useful insight into the textual metafunction:

[5.13]

i	**Non-manual**	brow raise			
	Manual	WALL	PT:LOC	LIST	DC:LIST-ON-WALL
	Textual	Theme:topical		Rheme	
		On the wall was a list.			

ii	**Non-manual**	brow raise		
	Manual	PT:PRO3SG	LIST	READ
	Textual	Theme:topical	Rheme	

He read the list.

iii	**Non-manual**	brow furrow
	Manual	CA:SCAN-LIST
	Textual	Rheme

(He) was scanning it,

iv	**Non-manual**	brow raise		
	Manual	THEN	ESCALATOR	DC:WALK-TO-ESCALATOR
	Textual	Textual Theme	Rheme	

then (he) walked to the escalator.

v	**Non-manual**	lips pouted; indirect gaze
	Manual	DC:TRAVEL-UP-ON-ESCALATOR
	Textual	Rheme

(He) idly travelled to the top of the escalator

vi	**Non-manual**	brow raise	headshake
	Manual	BUT	DC:WALK-AWAY
	Textual	Theme:textual	Rheme
		Given	New

but (he) didn't continue.

vii	**Non-manual**	brow raise		
	Manual	LATER	AT-LAST	REALISE
	Textual	Theme:text.	Theme:int.	Rheme

Then, (he) finally realised.

viii	**Non-manual**	brow raise	
	Manual	PT:PRO3SG	WALK
	Textual	Theme:topical	Rheme

He walked.

ix	**Non-manual**			brow raise				
	Manual	SECOND	FLOOR	HAVE	WHAT	MANNEQUIN		DC: MANNEQUIN-IN-PLACE
	Textual		Theme:topical				Rheme	
				Given			New	

The second floor has a mannequin.

x	**Non-manual**	brow raise	
	Manual	PT:PRO3SG	DC:BUMP-INTO-MANNEQUIN
	Textual	Theme:topical	Rheme

He bumped into the mannequin.

In this extended excerpt, it becomes quickly apparent that the signer is using various textual resources to maintain the flow of the discourse and to attribute prominence to its different parts. To begin exploring this in more detail, the different kinds of Theme (i.e. textual, interpersonal and topical) realized in each clause are summarized in Table 5.1.

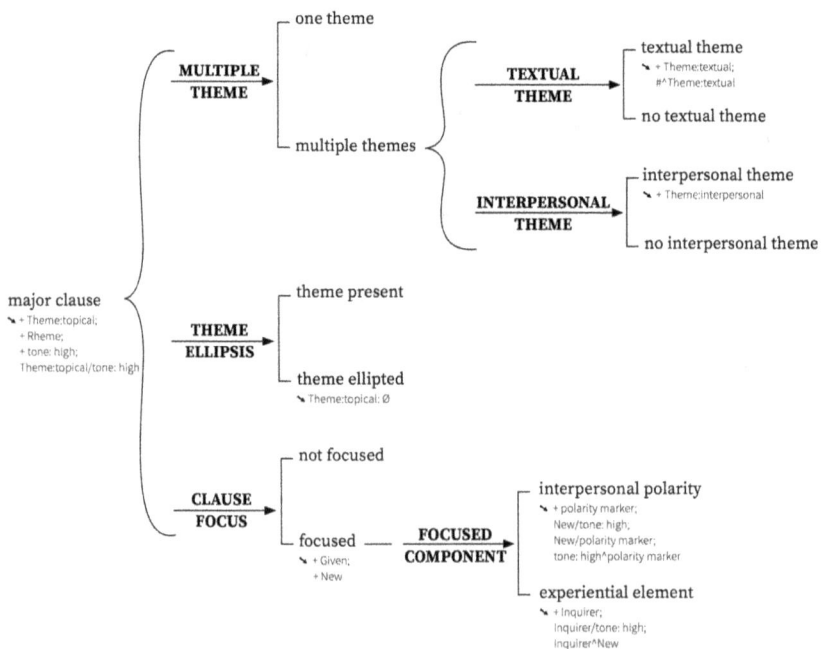

Figure 5.5 The textual systems of BSL.

Table 5.1 Realizations of different types of Theme in Excerpt 5.13 ('^' in the topical Theme column indicates that the realization was ellipted).

Clause number	textual Theme	interpersonal Theme	topical Theme
i	-	-	WALL PT:LOC
ii	-	-	PT:PRO3SG
iii	-	-	^PT:PRO3SG
iv	THEN	-	^PT:PRO3SG
v	-	-	^PT:PRO3SG
vi	BUT	-	^PT:PRO3SG
vii	LATER	AT-LAST	^PT:PRO3SG
viii	-	-	PT:PRO3SG
ix	-	-	SECOND FLOOR
x	-	-	PT:PRO3SG

The development of the discourse in Excerpt 5.13 suggests that the predominant focus centred on PRO3SG (i.e. pronominally referring to the actions of the observed protagonist). This begins from clause (ii) and then continues until clause (ix), wherein a new location is stated to 'situate' the next bout of actions enacted by the protagonist. Given that the topical Theme changes infrequently throughout these ten clauses, its realization is generally ellipted throughout. There are, however, two instances where this ellipsis can be examined further. In clauses (iii) and (v), constructed action (CA:SCAN-LIST) and a depicting construction (DC:TRAVEL-UP-ON-ESCALATOR) are used. In the former, the signer uses their own body as a representation of the protagonist, and in the latter, the protagonist is represented via the handshape of an extended upright index finger. Therefore, while not using a specific sign such as PT:PRO3SG prior to these constructions to overtly realize the topical Theme as a separate entity, the referent is nonetheless present through other embodied aspects. It must be remembered, though, that these are necessary components within such constructions: constructed action uses the signer's body as the representation of a Participant, and depicting constructions will 'depict' Participants by way of manual aspects (e.g. as alternative representations like in clause (v), as mimetic handling or mid-air tracing; see Emmorey, 2003). These clauses have been categorized as employing topical Theme ellipsis (particularly as the production of a manual sign to realize the topical Theme would have been possible in each).

Although topical Theme ellipsis is prominent throughout the excerpt, clause (viii) does show the realization of the topical Theme via PT:PRO3SG even though this did not change from previous clauses. An important differentiating factor to note here concerns the rhythm with which the clauses were produced. There was a noticeable pause between clauses (vii) and (viii) wherein the signer's hands returned to a more neutral position before continuing the dialogue. To again revisit the wave-like analogies used in this chapter, this may indicate the end of one wave of broad information and the start of a new wave (like what is seen in systemic functional literature regarding the hyperTheme; see, e.g., Figueredo, 2020). As such, although the topical Theme did not alter between these clauses, its deliberate inclusion can be argued to indicate the point at which a larger wave begins.

Instances of multiple Theme are also present in clauses (iv), (vi), (vii) and (viii) of the excerpt. In three of these instances, there are textual Themes to assist with the flow and connection of the overall dialogue, with THEN and LATER assisting the sequencing of actions and BUT representing an adversative relationship between the information offered in clauses (v) and (vi). Only one interpersonal Theme is noted in clause (vii), AT-LAST, and it appears in its expected syntagmatic position: prior to the topical Theme and after the textual Theme.

Clauses (vi) and (ix) demonstrate instances where the prominence and focus of the information shift from typical patterning seen in the other clauses. The glosses for these two clauses are expanded to show Given and New (which, for other clauses, would conflate with topical Theme and Rheme respectively). Both clauses demonstrate a distinction in what is focused on, with interpersonal negative polarity being the focus of the former (by using a headshake), and an experiential Participant being the focus of the latter (by using non-manual elements and realizing an Inquirer function as WHAT).

Before concluding, a productive element of BSL that is facilitated via the visual-spatial modality is worth noting, although not directly associated with any of the systems mentioned in this chapter. Between clauses (ix) and (x), the signer 'holds' the handshape of a depicting construction in position, specifically the left hand used to represent the position of the aforementioned MANNEQUIN. This remains in position as clause (x) is produced, as demonstrated in Figure 5.6.

The signer used their non-dominant hand to identify and place a referent for MANNEQUIN in the signing space, but rather than pointing and returning the hand to a neutral position, they held the referent in place. This was likely performed in anticipation of the Process realized in clause (x), wherein the

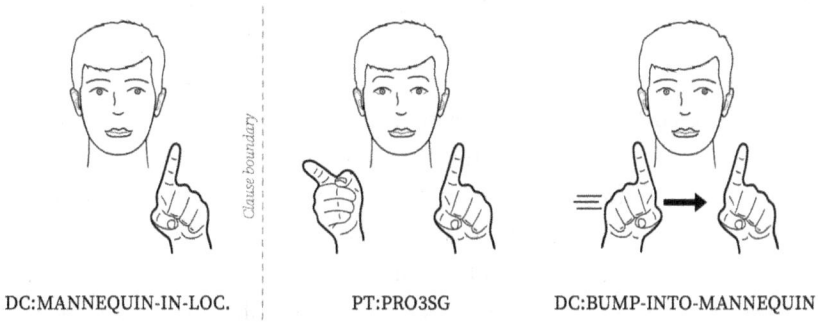

| DC:MANNEQUIN-IN-LOC. | PT:PRO3SG | DC:BUMP-INTO-MANNEQUIN |

Figure 5.6 An example of a held manual component from Excerpt 5.13.

protagonist (represented by a similar handshape on the signer's right hand) bumps into MANNEQUIN (via the right hand contacting the left hand at speed). This small instance demonstrates the ability to visually 'hold' meaning in place during production, and this may have consequences for the way that more complex stretches of BSL discourse are analysed from textual perspectives. This may even involve aspects of the logical metafunction (e.g. being able to 'hold' a clause or a part thereof while continuing to sign in a parenthetical manner, before returning to the held aspect).

Summary

Irrespective of the language used, texts are a web of interrelated threads, both within themselves and with regard to other texts out in the world. It is the observation of these instances via the lens of the textual metafunction that allows us to explore these webs. In this chapter, one of the core aspects of this metafunction – namely, the identification of information structure and its periodic or 'wave-like' patterning within the clause – has been introduced and exemplified for BSL.

The textual networks presented here provide a good point of departure for those wishing to explore how BSL functions in this regard at clause level. Through an understanding of the importance of Theme and Rheme, and their interrelations with aspects such as Given and New, the systems of MULTIPLE THEME, THEME ELLIPSIS and CLAUSE FOCUS can be used to interrogate the structure and development of BSL texts. Of course, this is not to say that these are the only systems that operate from a textual perspective. Given the complexity of the textual metafunction and its links to the interpersonal and ideational metafunctions overall (i.e. due to the 'enabling' nature of the textual metafunction), it is expected that there will be further developments to the systems offered here and their relationship to systems found at other strata. Furthermore, despite the correlations observed between realizations of textually functional components in BSL and other languages (e.g. the use of intonation, whether visual or verbal, to assist in marking topical Theme), the visual-spatial modality offers a layer of productive complexity that warrants further exploration from textual perspectives. That is, the ability for signs to persevere in the signing space while another articulator is producing meaning could lead to some unique textual observations. When this is combined with the possibility of two or more BSL users interacting within a shared signing space, this again expands the potential for cohesive techniques that are not necessarily seen in the oral-aural modality.

BSL has now been observed through three individual metafunctional lenses: the interpersonal (Chapter 3), the experiential (Chapter 4) and the textual. This has offered many perspectives in a deliberately segmented manner, but as described in Chapter 2, the metafunctions do not operate independently of one another. Rather, all metafunctions operate simultaneously in any given stretch of text, and the clause is often the locus where these metafunctions interact. It therefore now remains to combine these lenses and observe instances of BSL from this triple perspective.

6

Combining the Metafunctions: Analysing BSL from Three Perspectives

One of the many beneficial aspects of applying the broader systemic functional framework to language description and analysis is the holistic nature with which it approaches the phenomenon of social semiosis. As has been demonstrated in previous chapters, the meanings found in a linguistic system can be reliably split into several perspectives covering the exchange and negotiation of meaning (interpersonal; Chapter 3), the representation of experience (experiential/ideational; Chapter 4) and the broader organization and development of meaning over time (textual; Chapter 5). The layout of the book up to this point has deliberately split these metafunctions to provide separate in-depth explorations of each with regard to BSL. However, this should not be taken to imply that the meanings produced through different metafunctional lenses result in a 'one or the other' situation. As suggested in Chapter 2, these metafunctions operate simultaneously, leading to interactions and patterns of realization between them.

This chapter presents an analysis of an extended BSL text through the combination of the interpersonal, experiential and textual metafunctions. This is presented in three broad parts. To begin, a brief review on the theoretical importance of metafunctional simultaneity is presented. Then, a sample of BSL discourse is analysed with all three metafunctions addressed throughout. Finally, a summary of the patterning observed in the analysis is offered, with comparisons made to the typological insights of Matthiessen (2004b). A 'grand system network' is also schematized that demonstrates how each of the primary systems discussed in Chapters 3, 4 and 5 interrelate.

Unlike the previous three chapters, the current chapter is more 'applied' in its content. While appropriate theory is noted from the perspectives of SFL and sign linguistics, the goal of the current chapter is to demonstrate and elaborate on discoveries as they develop during analysis, as if it were being performed real-time. It is hoped that this will both offer insight into the semiotic richness of BSL and operate as a guide for how future analyses of BSL – and of other sign languages – could be enacted via systemic functional perspectives.

Metafunctional simultaneity

SFL is an approach that does not shy away from the complexities and intricacies of language when viewed as a social tool for making meaning. This ethos was introduced in Chapter 2 and exemplified in subsequent chapters, with attention paid to context, discourse semantics and their relationships with the lexicogrammatical stratum in BSL. While the metafunctions and their accompanying elements are indeed complex on their own, the social semiotic puzzle is not quite complete in its current state. It is now necessary to take each of these metafunctions and observe how they operate in tandem.

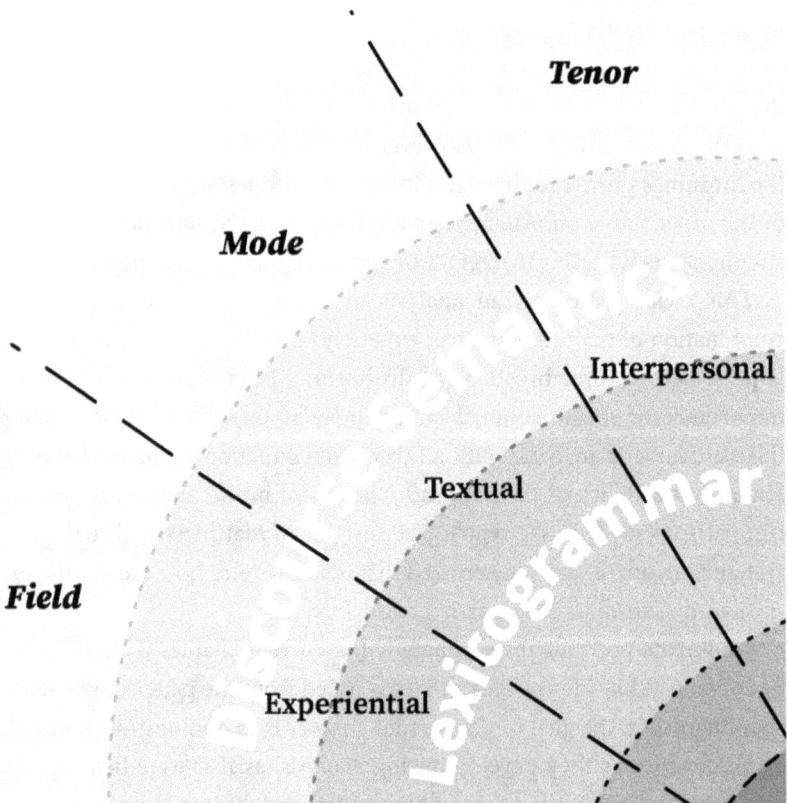

Figure 6.1 Metafunctions in a semiotic system.

As a reminder and as a visual guide, Figure 6.1 repeats what was introduced in Chapter 2. Within the broader representation of this schematized linguistic system is the idea that these different metafunctional tranches are distinct; yet, they nonetheless intertwine, both in instances of language and across a language as full system. In other words, linguistic realizations serve as a conduit for meaning as exchange (interpersonally), as representation (experientially) and as message (textually) at the same time.

Metafunctional simultaneity is one of the foundations of the systemic functional approach. For instance, from language development perspectives, Halliday (1975) notes that the ability to interweave and use each metafunction demonstrates that the language user has a functioning grasp of the language in use. Put another way, the language user has progressed in their knowledge and use of language as a full semiotic system, rather than as a symbolic system of one-to-one relationships between form and meaning. The importance of metafunctional simultaneity can also be understood from the perspective of text and genre. Martin (1992; referring to Pike, 1982) identifies 'the complementarity of perspectives' (p.548) wherein elements of structural realization from different metafunctions overlap and integrate with one another. More recently, Martin's (2010) notion of 'coupling' suggests that, in specific instances of language use, some functional elements may be regularly co-selected with others 'across strata, metafunctions, ranks, and simultaneous systems' (p.19). Thus, coupling presupposes simultaneous realizations of choices across metafunctions. Furthermore, Matthiessen (2004b) draws together observations from multiple systemic functional descriptions of language. In this wide-ranging account, metafunctional unification is noted: 'In any given language there will be systemic interactions across these major metafunctional systems, for example in the way that the system of MOOD relates to the system of THEME or the system of INFORMATION in the textual treatment of "wh-" interrogatives' (p.543).

With the above in mind, it is now possible to draw together the major lexicogrammatical systems for BSL across the interpersonal, experiential and textual metafunctions that have been presented in this work. This 'grand system network' is presented in Figure 6.2. For the sake of readability, each system is presented at its lowest form of delicacy and without realization statements, although their more elaborate forms can be found in their respective chapters in this book.

The unification schematized in Figure 6.2 argues that selections at clause rank occur across systems and thereby across metafunctions. A major clause will thus interpersonally select for MOOD, POLARITY, MODALITY and SOCIAL PROXIMITY,

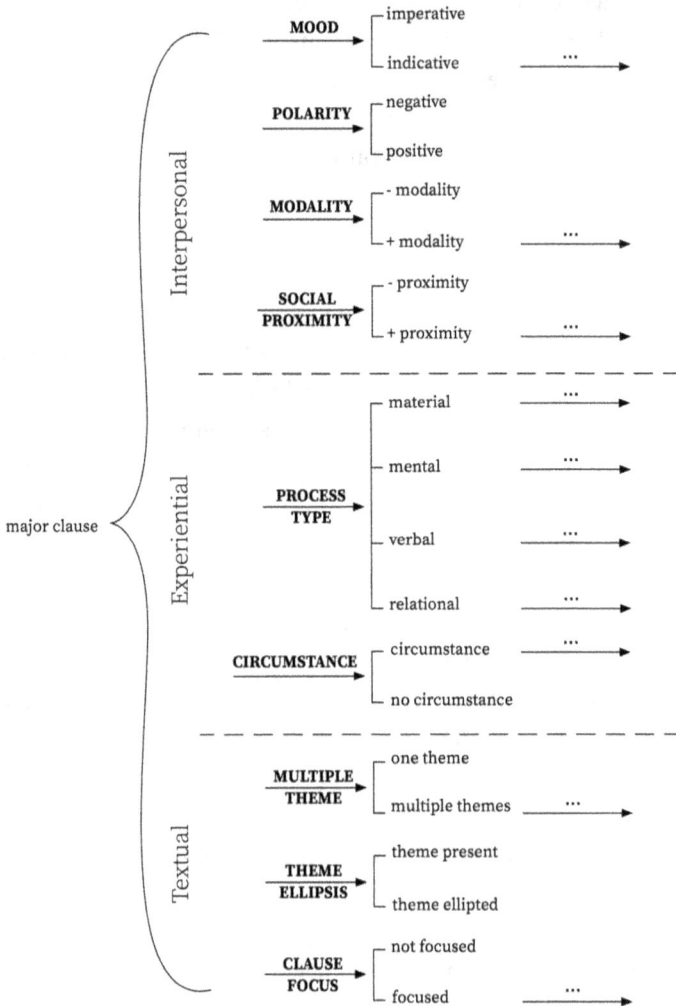

Figure 6.2 Lexicogrammatical systems in BSL across interpersonal, experiential and textual metafunctions.

as well as across the experiential systems of PROCESS TYPE and CIRCUMSTANCE, and the textual systems of MULTIPLE THEME, THEME ELLIPSIS and CLAUSE FOCUS (and, *ergo*, any subsequent systems at greater levels of delicacy). To investigate how these selections are made in BSL, and to understand the patterns of cross-metafunctional selections akin to Martin's (2010) suggestion of 'couplings', it is possible to analyse an extended excerpt of BSL dialogue from this triple perspective.

Analysing BSL via SFL: A full view

The remainder of this chapter will focus on a step-by-step analysis of BSL, using as its base an interaction drawn from the dataset employed in Chapter 5. Specifically, the excerpt used here was recorded just after the 'controlled' part of the data collection had finished. In this instance, both BSL users – who had known each other for many years – had been informed that the data collection had finished. However, the signers continued to converse following the topic of conversation from the preceding task (i.e. recounting actions from a cartoon that was observed by one of the signers). As the cameras were still recording at this point, I asked both signers if they would be happy for me to capture this additional data (with the ongoing caveat that any personally identifying or specific information for any parties would be pseudonymized), to which they both agreed.

In comparison to the other data that I had obtained from that recording session, this data is arguably a more 'natural' instance of BSL interaction. It is an informal dialogue between two friends, who rely on a significant amount of shared background knowledge and experiences of shared events to carry out the interaction. Immediately after I had informed both participants that the controlled portion of the recording had completed, the signer who had watched the cartoon (X) identified that one of the characters looked like a mutual acquaintance (R). The other signer (Y) attempts to recall who R is, and then they both briefly share memories of this person.

Given the length of this section of the interaction, Excerpt 6.1 is first displayed in a simplified clause-by-clause manner, with only manual, non-manual, spatio-kinetic values provided alongside broad translations. No metafunctional glossing is provided yet to allow the reader to become better acquainted with the text prior to its analysis.

[6.1]

X	Non-manual	brow raise
	Manual	MAN FROM CARTOON PT:DET -r- RESEMBLE
		The guy from that cartoon looks like 'R.'

X	Non-manual	brow raise
	Manual	PT:PRO2SG -r- REMEMBER
		(Do) you remember 'R?'

Y	**Non-manual**	brow furrow	
	Manual	-r-	WHO
		Who (was) 'R?'	

X	**Manual**	FROM	BIRMINGHAM
		('R' was) from Birmingham.	

[Y gazes away from X for a few seconds while thinking]

Y	**Non-manual**	head nod	
	Manual	REMEMBER	PT:PRO3SG
		(I) remember him.	

Y	**Spatio-kinetic**		slower hand movement
	Non-manual	brow raise	narrow eye aperture
	Manual	PT:POSS3SG BODY	LOVELY
		His body (was) really nice!	

X	**Non-manual**	head nod	
	Manual	HANDSOME	
		(He was) nice	

X	**N.-m.**	brow raise	head nod		brow raise	head nod
	Manual	BUT	REALLY	PT:PRO3SG	WHAT	IDIOT
		but, honestly, he (was an) idiot.				

[X and Y laugh for a few seconds]

X	**Non-manual**	brow furrow		
	Manual	PT:PRO3SG	NOW	WHERE
		Where (is) he now,		

X	**Non-manual**	brow furrow	
	Manual	WONDER	
		(I) wonder?	

Y	**Non-manual**	brow raise	different facial 'poses'; gaze at MIRROR location
	Manual	MIRROR PT:LOC	CA:LOOK-SEDUCTIVELY
		(He's) adoring himself in a mirror.	

Y	Non-manual	brow raise			
	Manual	OR	MAYBE	UNIVERSITY	GO
		Or maybe (he) went to university?			

X	Non-manual	headshake; brow furrow; lip pout	
	Manual	PT:PRO1SG	BELIEVE
		I (do)n't think (so).	

X	Non-manual		downturned lips; gaze at BOOK location
	Manual	BOOK PT:LOC	CA:PUSH-BOOKS-AWAY
		(He) wasn't fond of books!	

Excerpt 6.1 demonstrates a genuine informal interaction in BSL. Even at a surface level, it is clear to see that combinations of manual, non-manual and spatio-kinetic elements are required for successful meaning to be made. However, we can now break this interaction down further into tiers of interlinear glossing to see how the three metafunctions and their respective system networks presented in this book work together. Readers are recommended to have Figures 3.13, 4.11 and 5.5 accessible (i.e. the full interpersonal, experiential and textual systems networks of BSL) so that the explanations can be understood in the contexts of selections made in each network.

The analysis begins with Excerpt 6.1a, analysing the opening clause of the interaction:

[6.1a]

X	Non-manual	brow raise					
	Manual	MAN	FROM	CARTOON	PT:DET	-r-	RESEMBLE
	Interpers.						Predicator
	Experien.		Index			Aspect	Process:rel.
	Textual		Topical Theme				Rheme
		The guy from that cartoon looks like 'R.'					

The first clause functions to present a statement of fact. From the perspective of interpersonal MOOD, this is a move in which information is provided (i.e. [declarative]), rather than requesting (i.e. [interrogative]) or commanding (i.e. [imperative]). In terms of other interpersonal aspects, POLARITY selects for [positive] and MODALITY for [- modality], thereby resulting in a clause that is relatively unmarked. Only the Predicator is realized as a required functional element that permits this 'move' in the dialogue to be made.

Experientially, Excerpt 6.1a is analysed as a clause realizing a relational Process, specifically [relational: intensive] due to the attribution and association between the two expressed elements, MAN FROM CARTOON PT:DET and -r-. In general, most intensive relational Processes in BSL are expressed by the juxtaposition of two nominal groups without the realization of a verbal group, as detailed in Chapter 4. However, the meaning expressed in Excerpt 6.1a via RESEMBLE adds shades of indeterminacy to this clause. If RESEMBLE were not present, then the meaning realized would be one of the cartoon character being R. RESEMBLE thereby creates a similar functional link between the Index and Aspect as seen in other [relational: intensive] selections, but its inclusion indicates likeness rather than direct equivalency.

Textually, the clause in Excerpt 6.1a demonstrates a typically unmarked construction with the realization of topical Theme followed by Rheme. The boundary of these functional components occurs with the X's eyebrows shifting from a raised position to a neutral position. When viewed from intonational perspectives (i.e. at the phonological stratum), this suggests a shift in the (visual) intonational curve: the thematic information is 'highlighted' until the Rheme begins.

Overall, this first clause provides a good example of a 'typical' clause in BSL, in the sense of its communicative function and that it is mostly unmarked in its realization. Excerpt 6.1b, however, demonstrates two clauses with further levels of structural complexity:

[6.1b]

X				
Non-manual		brow raise		
Manual	PT:PRO2SG	-r-		REMEMBER
Interpers.				Predicator
Experien.	Senser	Phenomenon		Process:mental
Textual	Theme:top.		Rheme	
	(Do) you remember 'R?'			

Y			
Non-manual		brow furrow	
Manual	-r-		WHO
Interpers.			Predicator/Inquirer
Experien.	Index		Aspect
Textual	Theme:top.		Rheme
	Who (was) 'R?'		

In the first clause in Excerpt 6.1b, X wishes to confirm that the person being referred to is known by Y. To do this, Y is addressed through the pointing sign PT:PRO2SG. Then, X realizes the queried Participant, followed by the interpersonal Predicator co-occurring with raised eyebrows (or, in visual intonation terms, with a high tone). X's clause is therefore a move that selects for [interrogative: polar] in MOOD terms (i.e. asking Y to confirm or deny the proposition being put forward by X). Experientially, the clause realizes a mental Process, with the Participants organized into the one performing the action (i.e. the Senser) and the element that is 'sensed' (i.e. the Phenomenon). There is also a textually unmarked pattern of topical Theme and Rheme.

As X posed a question, Y's expected response from an interpersonal perspective would be expected to select a [declarative] MOOD structure. However, Y responds to X with another [interrogative], although different to that of X. Y is instead uncertain of who the person is, so Y attempts to elicit further information from X. This is achieved using furrowed eyebrows at the same time as a manual realization of an Inquirer function via WHO (which also conflates with the Predicator as it is the most interpersonally 'at risk' in the clause). In terms of MOOD, therefore, an [interrogative: elemental] is realized, distinct from X's [interrogative: polar] selection in the preceding clause.

In experiential terms, Y's clause is similar to Excerpt 6.1a in that an intensive relational Process is realized, although this follows the more typical realization pattern of Index and Aspect without an accompanying verbal group. Textually, Y's clause has an unmarked pattern, with the topical Theme having the same boundaries as the first experiential element in the clause.

Immediately after Y's request for clarification, X responds. This is shown in Excerpt 6.1c:

[6.1c]

X	**Manual**	FROM	BIRMINGHAM
	Interpers.	Predicator	
	Experien.	Aspect/Circumstance:location	
	Textual	Rheme	

('R' was) from Birmingham.

[Y gazes away from X for a few seconds while thinking]

Y	Non-manual	head nod	
	Manual	REMEMBER	PT:PRO3SG
	Interpers.	Predicator	
	Experien.	Process:mental	Phenomenon
	Textual	Rheme	

(I) remember him.

In the first clause of Excerpt 6.1c, X provides further information to fulfil Y's previous request. Starting this time with the textual metafunction, the relatively clear patterning of Theme-Rheme stops at this point. X ellipts the topical Theme, likely due to its recoverability within the context (e.g. as Y's inquiry concerned just one specific referent, its realization in this informal context may be viewed as redundant). Via a selection of [theme ellipted] THEME ELLIPSIS, then, only the Rheme is realized in this clause. Interpersonally, Y's clause is unmarked as information is being provided in a straightforward manner (i.e. a [declarative] selection in MOOD). Experientially, a [relational] selection is made from the system of PROCESS TYPE, with FROM BIRMINGHAM realizing a spatial location and thus acting as a [relational: circumstantial] selection. FROM BIRMINGHAM also represents the Aspect of the clause (without Index as the topical Theme was ellipted), aligning with the realization statement in RELATIONAL TYPE: Aspect conflates with Circumstance, which in this case relates to the experiential system of LOCATION.

After obtaining this clarification and taking a moment to think, the second clause in Excerpt 6.1c shows how Y successfully recalls R. Interpersonally and experientially, this clause is unmarked, other than Y's head nod appearing to add emphasis to the statement. Textually, Y also ellipts of the topical Theme, but this has nonetheless changed from R (in the preceding clause) to a self-referential topical Theme (i.e. PRO1SG). This is an instance that does not fully align with previous research. As noted in Chapter 5, topical Theme ellipsis seems to be favoured when the referent remains the same between clauses (Pfau and Bos, 2016). Additionally, from formal perspectives, ellipting a first-person singular subject pronoun is understood to be unfavoured (McKee et al., 2011).

An explanation for this can be posited from textual and experiential perspectives concerning relevance and recoverability. In Excerpt 6.1b, X produced REMEMBER and realized Y as the Senser via PT:PRO2SG. Given the short distance between the request and the response, it is still contextually clear that Y is the one who was asked to confirm their knowledge (i.e. to participate as Senser with regard to REMEMBER as a mental Process). Self-reference to re-identify the Senser may therefore be redundant in this context and, consequently, the topical Theme can be ellipted (as topical Theme and Senser conflate in this clause) due to ease of recoverability.

After Y successfully remembers who R is, the conversation continues with Y providing further commentary, as shown in Excerpt 6.1d:

[6.1d]

Y	Spatio-kinetic			slower hand movement
	Non-manual	brow raise		narrow eye aperture
	Manual	PT:POSS3SG	BODY	LOVELY
	Interpers.			Predicator
	Experien.	Index		Aspect
	Textual	Theme:topical		Rheme

His body (was) really nice!

X	**Non-manual**	head nod
	Manual	HANDSOME
	Interpers.	Predicator
	Experien.	Aspect
	Textual	Rheme

(He was) nice

X	**N.-m.**	brow raise	head nod		brow raise	head nod
	Manual	BUT	REALLY	PT:PRO3SG	WHAT	IDIOT
	Interp.				Inquirer	Predic.
	Exper.			Index		Aspect
	Text.	Theme:tex.	Theme:int.	Theme:top.	Rheme	
				Given		New

but, honestly, he (was an) idiot.

[X and Y laugh for a few seconds]

In the first clause of Excerpt 6.1d, Y offers a short elaboration on their previous statement by providing commentary on R's appearance. This first clause appears to be relatively simple in its composition, and through all three metafunctional lenses, there is no marking that has not been encountered in previous clauses (although the non-manual and spatio-kinetic productions accompanying LOVELY enhance the information provided, glossed as *really nice* rather than just *nice*).

X then follows Y's observation in the second clause of Excerpt 6.1d. The primary point of interest in this clause is its relative simplicity in comparison to the other clauses analysed so far. As the topical Theme had not changed since the previous clause, an expected selection of [theme ellipted] in THEME ELLIPSIS results in its omission (and, by extension, the omission of the experiential Index). Therefore, as X agrees with Y's observation, only the realization of an Aspect was needed, which carries a close experiential link with the previous Aspect (i.e. LOVELY and HANDSOME as near-synonyms). This is realized alongside a head nod to corroborate the agreement.

If the second clause presents relative simplicity, then the third clause of Excerpt 6.1d very much presents the converse. After providing agreement to Y's observation, X moves to offer further information as a caveat to this agreement, beginning with the adversative conjunction BUT. This is the first instance in the wider excerpt of a clause that starts with textual Theme made in the system of MULTIPLE THEME. Functionally, this presents a contrast between X's previous statement and the one that is about to be expressed. Furthermore, an interpersonal Theme expressing X's stance is realized and is located between the textual Theme and topical Theme, PT:PRO3SG.

Following the topical Theme, an interpersonal Inquirer function is realized via WHAT and co-occurs with raised eyebrows (i.e. a high tone). In the interpersonal system of MOOD, the Inquirer is added into the clause when the selection of [interrogative: elemental] is made, but this selection implies a non-manual realization of furrowed eyebrows (i.e. a low tone). Looking instead from a textual perspective, a [focused] selection is made in the system of CLAUSE FOCUS, whereby this manual and non-manual combination serves to heighten the newsworthiness of an experiential element, which in this case is the Aspect: IDIOT. In other words, the use of an interpersonal function with a 'non-congruent' non-manual production creates a textual shift in the boundary between Given and New so that an experiential function in the clause can be given prominence.

Prior to moving on from Excerpt 6.1d, it is important to identify – and reiterate – that not all parts of a clause will be relevant to each metafunction (at least not from the analytical perspectives offered in this work). This is quite clearly demonstrated by the extended use of partially glossed tiers in the clauses of Excerpt 6.1d. However, even this 'lack' of functions can be used to support other observations (e.g. that interpersonal meaning appears to be most at risk towards the end of a clause in BSL; cf. English clauses and Halliday and Matthiessen, 2014).

After X and Y's laughter at their comments regarding R, there is a moment in which their signing pauses. After a few seconds, X continues the dialogue as shown in Excerpt 6.1e:

[6.1e]

X	Non-man.	brow furrow		
	Manual	PT:PRO3SG	NOW	WHERE
	Interpers.			Inquirer/Predicator
	Experien.	Index	Circumstance:location (Phenomenon)	Aspect/Circumstance
	Textual	Theme:top.	Rheme	
		Where (is) he now,		

X	Non-manual	brow furrow
	Manual	WONDER
	Interpers.	Predicator
	Experien.	Process:mental
	Textual	Rheme
		(I) wonder?

Y	Non-man.	brow raise	different facial 'poses'; gaze at MIRROR loc.
	Manual	MIRROR PT:LOC	CA:LOOK-SEDUCTIVELY
	Interpers.		Predicator
	Experien.	Circ:accompaniment	Actor/Process:material/Circ.:manner
	Textual	Theme:topical	Rheme
		(He's) adoring himself in a mirror.	

The brief pause in signing acts as an indication of a textual shift from one phase of conversation to another (i.e. a shift in the hyperTheme; see Martin and Rose, 2007). This helps to explain the reintroduction of the previously realized topical Theme in this first clause of Excerpt 6.1e, as it re-establishes the dialogue after an interruption to the textual flow. Interpersonally, this first clause sees a conflation between the Predicator and the Inquirer, WHERE, and the use of furrowed eyebrows (i.e. realizing an [interrogative: elemental] selection from the MOOD network).

Experientially, though, two facets of X's first clause require further explanation. Firstly, a new timeframe of reference is introduced with a Circumstance of temporal location. Until this point in the dialogue, the temporal frame of reference was situated in the past, although this was principally implied through the Processes of accessing and describing memories, rather than overtly established using signs such as BEFORE. X's use of NOW shifts the temporal location to the present for any realized Processes from this point forward. Secondly, this first clause may also be analysed in an alternative manner, demonstrated using the second experiential gloss tier in parentheses. If this clause is understood to be 'standalone', it may be analysed as a clause selecting for [relational: circumstance] in PROCESS TYPE. If it is analysed in relation to X's following clause, it can be argued to realize a Phenomenon of the mental Process realized as WONDER. In other words, this second perspective suggests that [projecting] was selected from the experiential system of PROJECTION, such that X's first clause realizes a Participant of the following mental Process.[1]

The final clause in Excerpt 6.1e displays an instance of constructed action. During these instances, Y signs such that their actions are understood to be those of a Participant and not necessarily of themselves. If the embodied Participant (in this case, the Actor of a material Process) is understood in the context, the use of a separate sign (e.g. PT:PRO3SG) to identify the Participant may be ellipted. In the gloss of this final clause, this is why Actor is written in lighter text: it is present, but its realization is a result of the nature of constructed action requiring the signer to 'embody' a Participant, rather than expressing a separate sign. Otherwise, the remaining experiential functions that conflate at this point are more deliberate in their production – the Process is made clear through Y's actions, and the Circumstance is realized through Y's non-manual features, including their face and body posture.

The final bout of X and Y's interaction is analysed in Excerpt 6.1f.

[6.1f]

Y	Non-man.	brow raise			
	Manual	OR	MAYBE	UNIVERSITY	GO
	Interpers.		Modal		Predicator
	Experien.			Scope	Process:material
	Textual	Theme:text.	Theme:int.		Rheme
		Or maybe (he) went to university?			

X	Non-manual	headshake; brow furrow; lip pout	
	Manual	PT:PRO1SG	BELIEVE
	Interpers.		Predicator
	Experien.	Senser	Process:mental
	Textual	Theme:topical	Rheme
		I (do)n't think (so).	

X	Non-manual		downturned lips; gaze at BOOK location
	Manual	BOOK PT:LOC	CA:PUSH-BOOKS-AWAY
	Interpers.		Predicator
	Experien.	Goal	Actor/Process:material/Circ.:manner
	Textual	Theme:topical	Rheme
		(He) wasn't fond of books!	

In the first clause of Excerpt 6.1f, Y offers another possibility of what R may be doing, realizing a textual Theme selected from MULTIPLE THEME via OR. The topical Theme remains ellipted, as has been seen many times throughout the excerpt. Interpersonally, this first move is enacted by the realization of a Predicator function. MAYBE realizes a Modal function from the system of MODALITY, which in the subsequent system of MODALITY TYPE selects for [uncertainty] (and, in accordance with the realization statement, the Modal does not conflate with the Predicator). Also, B uses raised eyebrows throughout the clause, assisting both the realization of an [interrogative] MOOD selection and the abovementioned uncertainty levied via the Modal function (i.e. serving to increase Y's hesitation in expression). Experientially, the clause realizes a material Process, specifically one of motion towards a location. This is why UNIVERSITY is ascribed as a Scope rather than a Goal (i.e. it is not directly impacted by the material Process in question). Importantly, this clause is not expressing the specific displacement of the (ellipted) Actor, instead referring to the general idea of attending a university. As such, in the system of MATERIAL FOCUS, [physical displacement] is not selected, thereby explaining why a depicting construction of motion was not used in this clause.

X immediately dismisses Y's alternative proposal through the use of a [declarative] MOOD selection combined with a [negative] POLARITY selection. This latter is realized via the headshake co-occurring with the manual realization of the Predicator, BELIEVE. The additional aspects of visual prosody in this clause – the brow furrow and the lip pout – appear to lend further strength to the [negative] selection. These may also interact with MODALITY as in Y's previous clause and notions of certainty. As discussed in Chapter 3, instances such as these require further functional analysis. In this clause, there is no manual realization of a specific Modal function, but the non-manual elements of the production do appear to serve some manner of reinforcement.

In the final clause of this discourse, X provides reasoning for the preceding statement in an interestingly indirect way. This clause is analysed experientially as a material Process, realized by another instance of constructed action. Like in Excerpt 6.1e, X embodies the Actor and realizes the Process by the action of 'pushing books away' from them, with additional Circumstantial information provided by non-manual elements. Although this suggests the recounting of an action, it more accurately expresses that R did not appear to be someone who enjoyed studying, and would thereby be unlikely to follow Y's suggestion of going to university. This connotational meaning is expressed in the free translation of the final clause: *(He) wasn't fond of books!* This has been used rather than something more literal such as *He pushed books away with disdain* as this is not X's intended meaning. Consequently, the material Process is instead covertly expressing something akin to a mental Process with regard to a Participant's preferences and abilities. Such incongruency between meaning and realization (i.e. between selections at the discourse semantic stratum and expected selections at the lexicogrammatical stratum) suggests an occurrence of grammatical metaphor: 'the grammar symbolizing the semantics rather than directly realizing it' (Doran and Martin, 2020, p.11). Accurate analysis of grammatical metaphor in a language requires extensive amounts of data to further investigate patterns in incongruent realizations (Matthiessen, Teruya and Lam, 2010), but the datasets obtained in the current work do not provide enough instances of this semiotic phenomenon to comment further at this time. However, works such as Devrim (2015) can be consulted to provide further insight, as and when more comprehensive datasets of BSL usage are available.

Some preliminary descriptive motifs in BSL

The fourteen clauses analysed in this chapter have reconfirmed that there is a significant amount of description and investigation that can take place when language is viewed from systemic functional perspectives. The present analysis has only scratched the surface and there are still many opportunities for this data to be explored from complementary perspectives, such as analyses of functions at different lexicogrammatical ranks. To round off this chapter, though, I present considerations of how the three metafunctions work in tandem in BSL at clause rank, alongside comparisons to other systemic functional descriptions of languages.

In the concluding chapter of Caffarel, Martin and Matthiessen's (2004) collection of systemic functional descriptions of languages, Matthiessen (2004b) provides an extensive set of typological descriptive motifs. While the present work concerns only one language, the spirit of this concluding subsection intends to imitate that of Matthiessen's concluding chapter: to identify themes and patterns with regard to the systemic functional description and analysis of BSL. This includes realizational patterning seen in Excerpts 6.1a–f above and, where appropriate, comparisons with Matthiessen's typological identifications.

Matthiessen (2004b, p.540) notes a list of functions between languages that are deemed more variable or less variable, split between the interpersonal, experiential and textual metafunctions. When compared to what is presented in the current work, many of these less variable functions are identifiable within BSL. For instance, interpersonally, Matthiessen notes the Predicator function and the system of TONE as less variable. For BSL, it can be seen that the Predicator is a core aspect ensuring that the negotiation and exchange of meaning can proceed (i.e. via selections in the system of MOOD). Also, the manual sign realizing the functional Predicator is the epicentre for additional elements of communication to select further elements of negotiation at lower levels of delicacy (e.g. changes in eyebrow height, conflations of Predicator with Inquirer and so on). While not addressed in quite the same way in the present work, TONE is argued to have connections with the system of VISUAL PROSODY and its associated systems, as presented in Chapter 3. This is argued in the sense of being something that is phonologically and phonetically mediated – rather than being more overtly lexicogrammatical in its nature – yet still holding strong connections to the discourse semantic stratum and the interpersonal metafunction. While prosodic features can scope across a clause, the location in a BSL clause with the highest 'interpersonal risk' is towards the end of a clause. This suggests (using Matthiessen's terminology) that BSL is a language that employs juncture prosody via interpersonal closure, as can be seen in languages such as Japanese (Teruya, 2007).

From experiential perspectives, Matthiessen (2004b) notes that less variable functions include Processes and Participants. This is to be expected overall given that the core requirements when enabling experience via language would include the expression of the who and the what, and how these relate (as discussed in Chapter 4). Matthiessen notes that Process is generally realized within a verbal group, which holds true for the most part in BSL. However, it has been demonstrated that realizations of some relational Processes do not incorporate a verbal group. Instead, the realization of this domain of experience relies on a combination of syntagmatic order (e.g. Index is generally followed by Aspect); non-manual elements (e.g. Index tends to conflate with a higher eyebrow position or 'high (visual) tone'); interpersonal factors (e.g. Aspect tends to conflate with Predicator); and, depending on textual influences, the recoverability of previously stated Participants (e.g. the Index and topical Theme often conflate, and if the topical Theme undergoes ellipsis, then an Aspect-only clause can occur). In other selections of PROCESS TYPE, verbal groups are realized that conflate with the interpersonal Predicator.

An interesting departure from Matthiessen's (2004b) typological patterning concerning the experiential metafunction involves his identification of experiential iconicity (which arguably interacts with the textual metafunction, discussed shortly). He states two possible configurations with regard to the sequential expression of functional elements, the first being that they 'will appear in a sequence that reflects the order of the flow in the unfolding of a quantum of change – the flow of control or the flow of agency' (p.551). The second option is that 'experiential elements that are semantically closer to the Process will appear closer to it in sequence than elements that are less directly involved in it' (ibid.). However, in both choices, Matthiessen notes that this is 'only a default: it can easily be over-ridden by textual and interpersonal factors' (ibid.).

BSL appears to align more with the first kind of experiential iconicity noted above, but there are two further aspects to consider. Firstly, given that BSL and other sign languages rely on visual-spatial resources to enact successful communication, there is the potential for visual salience to influence the organization of the clauses (see Volterra et al., 1984). Napoli and Sutton-Spence's (2014) investigations on the sequencing of signs in forty-two sign languages noted the following, irrespective of formal grammatical or semantic relations: in clauses containing two nominal groups representing physical entities within the signing space (i.e. from a topographic perspective), the nominal group referring to bigger or generally more static objects is signed before smaller and/ or mobile objects. Putting grammatical aspects to one side momentarily, it is plausible that an explanation for this weighs more towards sensorial Gestalt psychological aspects in terms of visual perception (e.g. the figure-ground principle; see Peterson and Gibson, 1994) and attempts to transmit information as unambiguously as possible. In other words, setting up a context that starts with broader, larger or less mobile Participants, followed by smaller, more mobile or more detailed Participants, allows for easier understanding than if this order were reversed. The datasets used in the current work seem to support this notion, but elaboration and further exploration of this area are strongly encouraged.

Secondly, experiential configurations across a clause are tricky to identify due to the numerous conflations of experiential functions that may occur. For BSL, this is found within instances of constructed action and depicting constructions. As demonstrated in Excerpts 6.1e and 6.1f of the current chapter, and in Figure 4.4 of Chapter 4, it is possible for multiple experiential functions to be realized simultaneously via the various embodied articulators available to a signer, as well as the ways in which manual signs move and interact in the signing space. Although possible for clauses in BSL to use neither constructed action nor depicting constructions, their *simultaneity of expression* nonetheless presents a question that is not necessarily observed in systemic functional descriptions of spoken or written language. Work has begun on considering how such instances may be approached with systemic functional frameworks (e.g. Rudge, 2020), but far more work is to be done on this before firmer conclusions can be drawn.

Matthiessen's (2004) typological motifs concerning the textual metafunction are in-line with what is observed in this work for BSL. The functions of Theme and Rheme are viewed as typologically stable, with topical Theme identified positionally. The pairing of Given and New is also noted to broadly conflate with Theme and Rheme respectively, unless Given-New boundaries are shifted using more typically interpersonal aspects (e.g. the realization of an Inquirer function alongside raised eyebrows) or the use of visual prosody to modify information structure. Matthiessen also notes that 'the textual mode of expression is based on degrees of prominence' (p.548) and elaborates its manifestation by identifying three overall types: culminative placement (i.e. initial or final placement within a clause), prominence markers (i.e. an element or construction that is highlighted) and tonic prominence (i.e. major intonational pitch movement). For BSL, it is argued that all three of these may be observable. In terms of culminative placement, signs towards the start of the clause are thematic regardless of selections within MULTIPLE THEME. In terms of either prominence marking or tonic prominence, the abovementioned use of an Inquirer with raised eyebrows can be used to shift the typical Given-New boundary, as observed in the final clause of Excerpt 6.1d. The exact categorization depends on if this combination of manual and non-manual features is interpreted as an effect attributable to the lexicogrammatical stratum or the phonological stratum (relating back to issues discussed in Chapter 2).

Overall, it is fascinating to see this alignment between typological observations from nearly twenty years ago to current data for a language that operates in a different modality to those originally analysed. Through this brief set of comparisons, alongside the fuller investigations into each metafunction provided in Chapters 3, 4 and 5, this work has demonstrated the potential that awaits further study of BSL and other sign languages from systemic functional perspectives. This will be discussed and encouraged further in the following, final chapter.

7

Looking Back and Looking Forward

In the summer of 2017, I submitted for examination my PhD thesis containing the first publishable attempt at describing and analysing British Sign Language through the lens of Systemic Functional Linguistics. It was the result of three years of hard work, community engagement, and many, many ups and downs. The work acted as a 'proof of concept' that systemic functional description and analysis were not restricted to languages that use spoken and/or written modalities of expression. Although work had been done to an extent on Auslan prior to this (Johnston, 1996), this was nonetheless the first that did so with BSL *and* that provided a detailed look at how its metafunctional diversity could be realized in the form of system networks.

Flash forward to 2022, wherein I have kept one eye on this area of research while performing other research and activities in various academic roles. Through reading, researching, analysing, debating and countless cycles of trial and error, it has culminated here as the first publication offering detailed insight into the workings of BSL from an SFL perspective. This has grown in accuracy and scope from what was presented in my doctoral thesis, while maintaining and promoting the idea that sign languages are overdue for further recognition and investigation – from systemic functional perspectives and others, both inside of the linguistic sphere and beyond. The organization of this book is such that those without any specific knowledge of BSL or SFL should still be able to access most (if not all) of the content provided. It also enables those with knowledge of BSL and/or SFL to further investigate, problematize and hopefully build on what I have added to these domains of knowledge.

The contributions made in this work are defensible with regard to current levels of understanding in the fields of BSL and SFL. Nonetheless, this work forms just the beginning of the descriptive and analytical journey, due in some part to the levels of BSL data available and the 'workforce' in this area. Matthiessen (2009) helpfully provides insight into the time needed for systemic functional descriptions of languages and how these might be developed in present-day academia. He estimates that it might take nine years for a research group to create a substantial, in-depth functional description of a previously undescribed language. In the context of BSL, though, a different picture is presented. The descriptions and analyses produced here are a more-or-less sole endeavour without access to a dedicated research group, and progress on these areas has been impacted by the Covid-19 pandemic. These points are not raised here as excuses for deficits in the current offering. Rather, these are instead highlighted to reconfirm that there is still an extraordinary amount of insight regarding BSL that is ready and waiting to be explored.

This work is therefore presented from the dual perspective of being an original, timely contribution to multiple fields in and around linguistics, and as an overview that only touches on the surface of the semiotic potential of BSL. In Chapters 1 and 2, aspects were introduced and discussed, including a brief sociocultural history of BSL and of sign languages. An overview of systemic functional theory and its potential for combination with languages operating in the visual-spatial modality was also presented to allow readers to gain a fuller understanding of why this work was not only possible, but also necessary. In Chapters 3, 4 and 5, the interpersonal, experiential and textual metafunctions were explored, demonstrating via analyses of BSL data that a systemic functional description is possible. In other words, we can approach such descriptions through understanding BSL as a semiotic system that permits the negotiation of meaning and the representation of experience with variances in organization, structure and salience. These insights were drawn together in Chapter 6 to provide an overview of the simultaneous nature of the metafunctions in dialogic BSL interaction, in turn revealing preliminary interactions and patterning between metafunctions and how these align with prior typological perspectives. This latter point is also testament to systemic functional theorists present and past, and their cooperative development of systemic functional theory. The fact that typological observations from roughly two decades ago can securely align with a contemporary description of a language operating in the visual-spatial modality surely offers further support to the domain of systemic functionalism as a robust method of understanding language overall as a social semiotic system.

In addition, and while unfortunate to have to state, this work also presents significant usage-based evidence that (once again) confirms that BSL is a fully fledged semiotic system, and that it should be treated as such from within and beyond linguistic realms. To recall points made in Chapter 1, the study of sign languages remains small in comparison to the work that is performed on languages that are spoken and written, despite available evidence showing the worldwide use of sign languages spanning centuries (if not millennia). Through government policies and persisting ideologies, there remain problematic aspects regarding a perceived legitimacy of these languages in terms of their use and study. This ranges from tokenistic nods towards 'recognition', as seen in the UK's supposed acknowledgement – and overall resultant inaction – of BSL as an official minority language (Lawson et al., 2019), to institutions and sign language users around the world choosing not to use these languages due to the remnants of decisions and practices from the not-too-distant past (Reagan, 2019). Of course, each language user has their own freedom of linguistic expression, and may indeed choose to use other languages over sign languages for personal and/ or ideological reasons. However, those behind choices at institutional levels that overtly or covertly impede access and availability of these languages for others must be held to account so that positive change can be securely enacted.

With the previous paragraphs in mind, the final question that can be explored in this work is: 'Where can we go now?' The answers to this are manifold, which is one of the reasons why it has been such a pleasure and a privilege to lead this work into analysing and describing BSL from systemic functional perspectives.

To begin, it is possible to scrutinize the main unit of analysis used in this work so far: the clause. It was noted in Chapter 2 that this construct is viewed as the point of departure for a significant amount of meaning potential in systemic functional terms, but that it was also potentially problematic in the study of sign languages. As such, other approaches have used the clause as a base and have later developed concepts such as the 'clause-like unit' (CLU) to highlight distinctions seen in sign language expression when compared with spoken and/ or written expression (see Hodge and Johnston, 2014). Nonetheless, the current work has attempted to work with the notion of a clause as understood in systemic functional terms, and more specifically, how such a unit may be conceptualized within interpersonal, experiential and textual domains. This was also performed due to Matthiessen's (2004b) comment that

> languages tend to be more congruent in terms of systemic organization than in terms of structural organization and that within systemic organization they tend to be more congruent within systems of low delicacy and less congruent (more typologically varied) within systems of higher delicacy. [...] By mapping out the clause, we thus identify the most inclusive domain by reference to which we have to interpret the resources of lower-ranking units [and] we are likely to see most clearly in the clause the various fractal patterns that are manifested in the various ranking domains of the grammar.

(pp.656–7)

As noted in Chapter 6, the descriptions and analyses presented in this volume do bear typological similarity with what has been observed in other languages, at least at initial levels of systemic delicacy. Not only does this provide a base from which systems can be expanded and explored, but it also offers the opportunity to explore further lexicogrammatical ranks. Chapter 2 provided some insight into this by offering a rank scale for BSL, demonstrating how lower ranks may be delimited and investigated, including a more detailed breakdown of the morphological rank (compared to what is seen in other systemic functional descriptions of language) due to the multiple articulators used in BSL expression. The use and development of this lexicogrammatical rank scale, up to and including the creation of a function-rank matrix, is strongly encouraged.

Another area of study arises from the level of description presented in this work for each metafunction (i.e. in Chapters 3, 4 and 5). At each stage, I have noted that there are aspects that appear to be more 'stable' than others, and that questions and further pathways for investigation remain numerous. Some of the more pertinent questions will be explained in the following paragraphs, addressing each metafunction in turn. However, these are not addressed in any particular order of urgency or significance.

In interpersonal terms, the system networks created and presented in this work demonstrate how so-called 'initiating moves' through the MOOD system may be realized in BSL expression, alongside other interpersonally relevant systems such as POLARITY and MODALITY. From this base, there are a variety of further pathways. Firstly, the congruent or 'expected' moves that follow the initiating move can be investigated (e.g. an initiating move selecting for [interrogative: elemental] may have a [declarative] as an expected following move), as can further impersonal moves that may precede or follow (see Martin, 2018). Secondly, the networks that are presented in Chapter 3 may be expanded on substantially, such as exploring further levels of delicacy following an [imperative] selection in MOOD, and similar expansions on the system of MODALITY TYPE. These would likely be assisted by a third area of investigation, namely more detailed descriptions at lower linguistic strata (e.g. phonology and phonetics). This includes exploring the system of VISUAL PROSODY further with regard to how multiple articulators can combine specific values of expression (e.g. eyebrow height, facial expression, eye aperture, torso tilt/lean and so on) to create nuanced selections in lexicogrammatical systems.

Fourthly, the system of POLARITY would benefit from insights at levels below the clause (i.e. at group or word rank). It was established in Chapter 3 that a headshake as a non-manual marker is a necessary feature for realization of [negative] selections of POLARITY. However, it was also alluded to that aspects of polarity occur within individual signs or groups of signs, such as phonological modifications to 'positive' signs to make them 'negative' (e.g. HAVE to HAVE-NOT). These instances offer various opportunities to explore how the division of grammatical labour is shared at different ranks in BSL (and, in turn, adding to the previously mentioned suggestion of the development of a function-rank matrix).

Finally, the system of SOCIAL PROXIMITY requires further data to be elaborated. In particular, data is needed to understand the distinctions between topographic and arbitrary signing space in BSL, such that confusion and ambiguity may be reduced in this system. At present, referring to a physically higher referent (topographic) or using the 'high plane' to designate an imbalance in interpersonal proximity (arbitrary) remains tricky to differentiate without additional contextual or co-textual cues.

Turning to the experiential metafunction, research pathways are also available aside from extensions of the systems schematized towards the end of Chapter 4. In particular, the experiential domain of relational Processes would benefit from further data and analysis of clause types, alongside the appropriacy of nomenclature for Index and Aspect, and the potential for additional functional components. There is also the opportunity for CIRCUMSTANCE TYPE to be expanded with further kinds of Circumstance beyond the four presented in this work, as is the potential for additional Process types to be considered. To reiterate what was discussed in Chapter 4, systemic functional descriptions of other languages often include behavioural and existential Processes in systems of PROCESS TYPE. There is certainly a likelihood that such Processes can be found in BSL, too, but current datasets do not permit enough clarity to allow for supportable conclusions via cryptogrammatical comparison (i.e. reactances, agnation and enation). Finally, the experiential perspective provided in this work offers a transitive view of experience, leaving the ergative perspective mostly untouched (i.e. notions of agency, medium, and so on, across Process types). Some insight into this experiential model is provided in Rudge (2018), but it is yet to be covered in the same level of depth as that seen for transitivity.

In terms of textual concerns, further exploration should address a metafunction that was not addressed here – the logical metafunction, covering the 'complexing' of multiple lexicogrammatical units in terms of their relative status (taxis) and their linked meaning (logico-semantics). While the textual metafunction focuses instead on aspects including information prominence and the overall logogenesis of text, both this metafunction and the logical metafunction would benefit from investigations beyond a clause-by-clause analysis. As noted in various works exploring the textual metafunction, such as Figueredo (2020), the textual metafunction can expand from considerations of Theme to broader developmental aspects across longer texts encompassing macroTheme and hyperTheme. These latter cannot be fully explored if focusing on individual clauses, as performed in this work. It should also be noted that work regarding the logical metafunction in Auslan is explored by Johnston (1996) who notes that the logic of clauses is 'linked in intricate ways by prosody, sequence, semantics and placement' (p.30). The notion of 'placement' is one that has not been covered in much depth in the present work, but it is important to note here that the signing space plays an essential part in this latter metafunction (since the placement of aspects in the signing space can create both status- and meaning-based connections). While little investigation has yet to take place in this area, it is certainly one that will provide fascinating insight into the way that a visual-spatial language can create extensive, rich meaning.

Questions also remain that cannot yet be confidently attributed to a particular metafunction. For instance, there are instances from the datasets used in this work akin to Excerpts 7.1 and 7.2 below:

[7.1]

L	**Non-manual**	brow raise		head nod
	Manual	PT:PRO3SG	SAD	PT:PRO3SG
	Interpersonal		Predicator	?
	Experiential	Index	Aspect	?
	Textual	Theme:topical	Rheme	?
		He was sad.		

[7.2]

T	**Non-manual**	brow furrow			
	Manual	WHERE	PT:POSS1SG	WALLET	WHERE
	Interpersonal	?			Inquirer
	Experiential	?		Index	Aspect
	Textual	?		Theme:topical	Rheme
		Where (is) my wallet?			

In both excerpts, one sign in the clause is expressed twice, in either clause-initial or clause-final position. This patterning is noted in sign linguistics literature as a way of highlighting topical focus, providing emphasis, or facilitating referential clarity. Sutton-Spence and Woll (1999) refer to this effect in BSL as 'pronoun copy' which is found in emphatic statements and may be accompanied with non-manual expression (e.g. a co-occurring head nod, as seen in Excerpt 7.1). Work in other sign languages, such as Jantunen's (2007) investigation of Finnish Sign Language (FinSL), names this effect as 'double-indexing': 'an optional pragmatic means which signers use to increase textual cohesion within a sentence' (p.13). In Norsk Tegnspråk (NSL or Norwegian Sign Language) similar instances are viewed as a method of discourse management and working with conversational turns (see Ferrera, 2020).

From the perspectives offered in this work, the functions of these repeated manual signs are not entirely clear, hence the use of question marks in Excerpts 7.1 and 7.2. These are discussed in the following paragraph. To clarify, the repeated sign is identified in clause-final position in Excerpt 7.1 and clause-initial position in Excerpt 7.2 because, based on what has been presented in this book, these appear to be the marked additions to the clause (e.g. interpersonally, an Inquirer function is expected to be realized in clause-final position).

When these excerpts are analysed using the insights offered in this work alone, the repeated sign in Excerpt 7.1 carries no interpersonal function. As such, it may fulfil a function from other interpersonal perspectives, such as APPRAISAL (Martin and White, 2005). The repeated sign in Excerpt 7.2 appears to echo the interpersonal Inquirer function, but this is not to say that there are two separate Inquirer functions being produced in one clause. Viewed experientially, both excerpts (and similar instances found in the dataset) realize a relational Process; thus, the repeated sign echoes one of the two possible Participants: Index or Aspect. However, they do not immediately appear to realize any additional experiential meaning. From textual perspectives, Excerpt 7.1 echoes the topical Theme at the end of the clause, but this repetition does not function as part of the Theme (i.e. it occurs within the Rheme). For Excerpt 7.2, as WHERE is placed clause-initially, this appears to impact the typical Theme-Rheme status of the clause, giving a level of prominence and focus to the Inquirer function (i.e. the first WHERE realizes topical Theme, with the remaining signs realizing the Rheme). This may resonate with the textual system of CLAUSE FOCUS as presented in Chapter 5.

Beyond individual metafunctions, and prior to drawing this work to a close, there are a few final suggestions for further exploration that can be highlighted. Perhaps most obviously, there is the application of this work to other sign languages, many of which have been mentioned as points of comparison throughout this work but have yet to be investigated using systemic functional frameworks. Some preliminary work has appeared with regard to describing Auslan from systemic functional perspectives (Johnston, 1996), and more recently, work has observed the development and acquisition of Flemish Sign Language via systemic functional theory (Wille et al., 2018). However, descriptions such as those that are presented in this book are yet to appear, although there are numerous works that focus on the formal and/or syntagmatic rather than the functional/paradigmatic (as noted in Chapters 1 and 2). It is hoped that the current work can be used as a basis from which other sign languages can be analysed and described (i.e. via transfer comparison in the visual-spatial modality in the first instance, and then leading to more glottocentric yet visually motived descriptions). To stipulate again, these comments are not intended to be seen as detractions from other approaches, and neither should the work presented here be taken as an iron-clad description of how BSL *should* be used. Rather, it is another interpretation to add to the growing body of knowledge on sign languages and on communication from social semiotic perspectives.

Tangentially, there is also a growing body of literature in systemic functionalism that addresses the semiosis via embodied communication, such as through the use of manual/co-speech gesture, eye gaze and so on (see, e.g., Ngo et al., 2021). There are many similarities that can be drawn between these areas of investigation and that which is presented in this work, given that the expression of BSL is generally 'restricted' to the visual-spatial modality. Although not evidenced explicitly in this work, other research and teaching that I have performed during the creation of this book has demonstrated that there are many possibilities for these two fields to work with one another, and that the methods of analysis used in each can be mutually beneficial regarding description, analysis and application.

Finally, it is hoped that this work can be used to promote the social and ethical necessity for BSL recognition and use, with more than just a token 'nod' in terms of its status in law. Other than reinforcing that BSL is a fully fledged language, there are insights that can be used here in the teaching and assessment of BSL, including the development of new materials that can be employed alongside those that are currently used in sign linguistics and sign language education. Cumulatively, this can provide BSL learners and users with alternative perspectives, and provide the deaf community with a description of a language that is visuocentric at its core, rather than attempting to create a 'best fit' of a sign language into a spoken language model of description. Although preliminary, this work presents one collective step further towards a way of understanding sign languages as semiotic systems in their own right.

Notes

Chapter 1

1 Available from: https://bda.org.uk/
2 Available from: http://www.bdhs.org.uk/
3 Available from: https://www.ucl.ac.uk/british-sign-language-history/
4 Available from https://www.ucas.com/
5 The BSL signbank can be accessed here: https://bslsignbank.ucl.ac.uk/
6 'Phonology' in the current context may appear to be a misnomer, given that phonology is often linked to expression in spoken language (as graphology is to expression in written language). However, this term is adopted throughout contemporary sign linguistics research. Sign language phonology is taken in the sense that 'signs can be constructed of form elements which are meaningless in themselves, but which have the capacity to distinguish meaning' (Van der Kooij and Crasborn, 2016, p.275). As such, 'phonology' here is understood in a modality-independent sense.
7 A sign name is a sign used to refer to a specific person, rather than fingerspelling that person's 'hearing' name. Sign names may reflect a physical trait of a person, a habit, a profession and so on. See Day and Spence (2010) for further discussion.
8 Hodge and Johnston (2014) also identify a category of 'non-lexical' signs which have 'very little conventionalization or specification of form and meaning' (p.267), such as 'manual and non-manual gestures' (ibid.). While I agree that this serves as an important distinction, I have chosen not to include this category in the current work as it leads to several potentially arbitrary dismissals of semiotic data. This will be clarified in Chapter 2, within the discussion of the sign-gesture split and the more recent notion of the 'semiotic repertoire' (Kusters et al., 2017).

Chapter 2

1 Fawcett (2008) offers an alternative perspective on metafunction in the Cardiff Grammar tradition.
2 The motivations for paradigmatic distinctions – the choices in system networks – are strongly related to fundamental concepts proposed by Whorf (1945) and later extended by Gleason (1965), including cryptogrammar, reactance, agnation

and enation. From a simplified perspective, these concern how the comparison of lexicogrammatical instances (e.g. clauses) results in patterns and distinctions, revealing information about underlying or 'covert' linguistic structures and categories (see Quiroz, 2020, for further introductions to these concepts, and Davidse, 2019, for deeper exploration). This analytical perspective has been employed in the analysis of BSL data and underpins the system networks presented in this work.

3 Following Cormier et al.'s (2017) annotation conventions, the depicting construction could be written as DESW(FLAT-HORI)-MOVE:CAR-PASSES-QUICKLY. This encodes further information such as the representation of a whole entity, the handshape and orientation, and the type of movement. For brevity, focus and accessibility, the present work does not employ these exact conventions, although the author acknowledges both the usefulness of these conventions and the potential for reduction in productive clarity.

4 'Word' is used in the systemic functional sense as a component of a dimension in a semiotic system (i.e. as a structural unit in a rank scale, below the rank of group and above the rank of morpheme; see Matthiessen, 2004a; Matthiessen, Teruya and Lam, 2010). This is not a terminological oversight, nor is it intended to equate the 'words' of a spoken or written language as identical to the 'signs' in a sign language.

5 One possible way of resolving this difficulty would be to revisit the model of stratification used as a theoretical primitive for this study (see Figure 2.1), and to reconsider (a) the number of strata used and (b) whether the stratal boundary between lexicogrammar and phonology is necessary. (Thanks are given to the reviewers of an earlier draft of this work for highlighting this potential pathway.)

6 Distinctions are nonetheless possible, even within this more holistic approach, such as the elements of embodied communication that are semiotic (i.e. meaning-bearing) or somatic (i.e. physical, perhaps involuntary, motion; see Martin and Zappavigna, 2019).

Chapter 3

1 While clearly an important area for future research, this book does not cover the complementary interpersonal discourse semantic systems found within Appraisal Theory (see, e.g., Martin and White, 2005).

2 Many of the systems provided in this and the following chapters were discussed in Rudge (2018). However, further data have helped to refine and elaborate on those systems, particularly in terms of the functions observed, realization statements and 'points of departure'. This iterative cycle of analysis and fine-tuning is one of the aspects that makes this kind of work so interesting, so I hope that readers will be encouraged to use this work to partake in this cycle!

3 All data has undergone pseudonymization: all participants are ascribed a letter and any names, signed or fingerspelled, are changed. Words in parentheses in the English tiers of excerpts are not overtly signed but are nevertheless required for the free translation to make sense.

4 These can also be accompanied by 'tilts' of the head and changes in eye aperture, although this latter point may be argued as a physiological constraint: it is possible to widen or squint your eyes without moving your eyebrows, but extremely difficult to raise or furrow your eyebrows without widening or squinting your eyes.

5 Unlike third-person singular pronouns in English, BSL does not encode gender in pointing (i.e. PT:PRO3SG in Excerpt 3.4 is neutral). However, the English translation gives a specific gender based on the communication from which the excerpt is drawn.

6 Non-manual features that scope across manual signs, such as those in Excerpts 3.4 and 3.5, may also realize meanings across metafunctions (e.g. realizing an experiential sense of heightened confusion, uncertainty or shock; textual prominence; etc.). Interpreting visual prosody is not an exact science, and what I offer in this work is performed to the best of my ability, but it remains a fruitful area of investigation.

7 A forward slash (/) between two elements in a realization statement indicates the simultaneous production of these elements. For instance, in a polar interrogative, the Predicator is realized at the same time as a high phonological tone, typically with raised eyebrows.

8 For this instance, I communicated with the signer to confirm whether my interpretation of their uncertainty was correct. The signer confirmed that this was the case, although it is understandable that not every single instance like this can be confirmed as such.

9 The realization statement for 'portraying' in this figure shows only eye gaze, although other non-manual features may also 'point' in that direction (e.g. head tilt, torso and so on).

Chapter 4

1 The final of these four domains of experience differs slightly from that presented in Halliday and Matthiessen (1999): 'expressing' replaces 'saying' because 'saying' is proposed here as a sub-type of experience (see Figure 4.1). 'Expressing' is also argued to be distinct from 'sensing': 'expressing' is concerned with projections of external content, whereas 'sensing' concerns projections of internal content.

2 In practice, subtle distinctions in functional identification as seen here and in broader transitivity analyses often lead to levels of indeterminacy. This is explored

by Gwilliams and Fontaine (2015) who propose a more multidimensional approach to such analyses. For the purposes of this work, I have followed a one-dimensional classification for ease of exemplification and comprehension, although I welcome alternative interpretations.

3 Sayer is used in this work to provide a point of comparison to similar system networks in other systemic functional descriptions of language (e.g. English; Halliday and Matthiessen, 2014), and is not used as an oversight. While BSL is not 'said' *per se*, SAY is sometimes used in BSL when the associated Verbiage refers to content that was originally signed.

4 Prior to both 'mental' and 'verbal' selections would be PROCESS TYPE, as seen in the material system network in Figure 4.6 above. This has been omitted from this figure to save space and improve readability.

5 SFL-based descriptions of languages like English (Halliday and Matthiessen, 2014) have numerous participants in relational processes when compared to what is presented here for BSL (e.g. Carrier, Attribute, Token, Value, etc.). This is not to say that such complexity is not found in BSL, but a binary participant distinction of 'identified thing' (Index) and 'associated thing' (Aspect) is sufficient at these early stages of description and analysis.

6 HAVE accounted for almost all realizations of the possessive relational process in the dataset used for this chapter, but OWN was also observed in one instance in similar sense and structure.

7 It is also worth noting that when these circumstances are realized by lexicogrammatical elements indicating a point in or span of time, it also temporally situates the associated processes and participants (or, in more formal terms, it sets up the tense of the clause). This effect can scope across long stretches of discourse, usually until another temporal sign is expressed that then 'shifts' the temporal location/tense of the clause.

8 There is the possibility of Scope conflating with, or being instead ascribed as, Circumstance:location, depending on whether FRANCE is regarded as a non-essential component in the context of GO.

Chapter 5

1 For a succinct visual representation of this 'wave-like' metaphor, see Figure 5.1 of Figueredo (2020).

2 © Tiger Aspect Productions.

3 The dataset suggests that those who regularly ellipted topical Theme tended to be younger, but this is offered cautiously as the dataset did not contain a demographically representative sample of BSL users, such as samples observed in more sociolinguistic studies (see Schembri and Lucas, 2015).

4 The realization statement for 'focused' indicates the addition of Given and New to the clause. In reality, Given and New will be present in all major clauses from a textual perspective, but are added here to highlight that there are specific interactions with these components and others in the sub-system FOCUSED COMPONENT.

Chapter 6

1 In this second interpretation, the position of these two clauses can be reversed with the same overall meaning produced. When inquiring with the signer during the analysis phase, X noted that if they were in a more formal context, they would have been more inclined to sign WONDER first, followed by PT:PRO3SG NOW WHERE. This effect appears to be above the level of the clause and more closely concerning the logical metafunction (see, e.g. Chapter 7 of Halliday and Matthiessen, 2014) which goes beyond the scope of this work.

References

Baker, A., B. van den Bogaerde, R. Pfau and T. Schermer, eds (2016), *The Linguistics of Sign Languages: An Introduction*, Amsterdam: John Benjamins.

Barberà, G. (2014), 'Use and functions of spatial planes in Catalan Sign Language (LSC) discourse', *Sign Language Studies*, 14 (2): 147–74.

Bartlett, T. (2018), 'Positive discourse analysis', in J. Richardson and J. Flowerdew (eds), *The Routledge Handbook of Critical Discourse Analysis*, 133–47, London: Routledge.

Batterbury, S. C. E. (2012), 'Language justice for sign language peoples: The UN Convention on the rights of persons with disabilities', *Language Policy*, 11 (3): 253–72.

Batterbury, S. C. E., P. Ladd and M. Gulliver (2007), 'Sign language peoples as indigenous minorities: Implications for research and policy', *Environment and Planning A*, 39 (12): 2899–915.

Berry, M. (1981), 'Towards layers of exchange structure for directive exchanges', *Network*, 2: 23–32.

Bianchini, C. S., L. Chèvrefils, C. Danet, P. Doan, M. Rébulard, A. Contesse and D. Boutet (2018), 'Coding movement in sign languages', *Proceedings of the 5th International Conference on Movement and Computing (MOCO'18)*: 1–8.

Börjars, K. and K. Burridge (2010), *Introducing English Grammar*, 2nd edn, London: Hodder Education.

Bragg, D., O. Koller, M. Bellard, L. Berke, P. Boudreault, A. Braffort, N. Caselli, M. Huenerfauth, H. Kacorri, T. Verhoef, C. Vogler and M. Ringel Morris (2019), 'Sign language recognition, generation, and translation: An interdisciplinary perspective', *The 21st International ACM SIGACCESS Conference on Computers and Accessibility (ASSETS '19)*, 16–31, New York: Association for Computing Machinery.

Brien, D., ed. (1992), *Dictionary of British Sign Language/English*, London: Faber and Faber.

British Deaf Association (2019), *Help and Resources for Sign Language*. Available online: https://bda.org.uk/help-resources/#statistics (accessed 15 November 2021).

Butler, C. S. (2003), *Structure and Function: A Guide to Three Major Structural-Functional Theories*, Amsterdam: John Benjamins.

Caffarel, A. (2006), *A Systemic Functional Grammar of French: From Grammar to Discourse*, London: Continuum.

Caffarel, A., J. R. Martin and C. M. I. M. Matthiessen (2004), *Language Typology: A Functional Perspective*, Amsterdam: John Benjamins.

Caudrelier, G. C. (2014), *The Syntax of British Sign Language*, MA dissertation, Lancashire: University of Central Lancashire.

Centre for Deaf and Hard of Hearing People (2020), *Where Is the Interpreter Campaign*. Available online: http://cfd.org.uk/where-is-the-interpreter-campaign/ (accessed 7 May 2020).

Christie, F. (2004), 'Systemic functional linguistics and a theory of language in education', *Ilha Do Desterro*, 46: 13–40.

Cormier, K., D. Quinto-Pozos, Z. Sevcikova and A. Schembri (2012), 'Lexicalisation and de-lexicalisation processes in sign languages: Comparing depicting constructions and viewpoint gestures', *Language and Communication*, 32 (4): 329–48.

Cormier, K., S. Smith and M. Zwets (2013), 'Framing constructed action in British Sign Language narratives', *Journal of Pragmatics*, 55: 119–39.

Cormier, K., J. Fenlon and A. Schembri (2015), 'Indicating verbs in British Sign Language favour motivated use of space', *Open Linguistics*, 1: 684–707.

Cormier, K., S. Smith and Z. Sevcikova-Sehyr (2015), 'Rethinking constructed action', *Sign Language and Linguistics*, 18 (2): 167–204.

Cormier, K., J. Fenlon, S. Gulamani and S. Smith (2017), *BSL Corpus annotation conventions (Version 3.0)*, London: Deafness Cognition and Language (DCAL) Research Centre, University College London.

CRIDE (Consortium for Research in Deaf Education) (2018), *CRIDE Report on 2018 Survey on Educational Provision for Deaf Children*. Available online: https://www.ndcs.org.uk/media/4722/cride-2018-uk-wide-report.pdf (accessed 15 November 2021).

Dachkovsky, S., C. Healy and W. Sandler (2013), 'Visual intonation in two sign languages', *Phonology*, 30 (2): 211–52.

Davidse, K. (2019), 'Systemic functional linguistics and the clause: The experiential metafunction', in T. Bartlett and G. O'Grady (eds), *The Routledge Handbook of Systemic Functional Linguistics*, 79–95, London: Routledge.

Day, L. and R. Sutton-Spence (2010), 'British sign name customs', *Sign Language Studies*, 11 (1): 22–54.

De Meulder, M., J. J. Murray and R. McKee (2019), 'Introduction', in M. De Meulder, J. J Murray and R. McKee (eds), *The Legal Recognition of Sign Languages: Advocacy and Outcomes Around the World*, 26–43, Bristol: Multilingual Matters.

Devrim, D. Y. (2015), 'Grammatical metaphor: What do we mean? What exactly are we researching?', *Functional Linguistics*, 2 (3): 1–15.

Dick, A. S., S. Goldin-Meadow, A. Solodkin and S. L. Small (2012), 'Gesture and the developing brain', *Developmental Science*, 15 (2): 165–80.

Doran, Y. J. and J. R. Martin (2020), 'Describing languages, understanding language', in J. R. Martin, Y. J. Doran and G. Figueredo (eds), *Systemic Functional Language Description: Making Meaning Matter*, 1–21, Oxford: Routledge.

Earis, H. and K. Cormier (2013), 'Point of view in British Sign Language and spoken english narrative discourse: The example of "The Tortoise and the Hare"', *Language and Cognition*, 5 (4): 313–43.

Eggins, S. (2004), *An Introduction to Systemic Functional Linguistics*, 2nd edn, London: Continuum.

ELAN (Version 5.9) (2020), *Computer Software*, Nijmegen: Max Planck Institute for Psycholinguistics. Available online: https://archive.mpi.nl/tla/elan (accessed 15 November 2021).

Emmorey, K. (2003), *Perspectives on Classifier Constructions in Sign Languages*, Mahwah, NJ: Lawrence Erlbaum.

Everett, D. L. (2017), 'Grammar came later: Triality of patterning and the gradual evolution of language', *Journal of Neurolinguistics*, 43: 133–65.

Fawcett, R. (2008), *Invitation to Systemic Functional Linguistics through the Cardiff Grammar*, 3rd edn, London: Equinox.

Fenlon, J., K. Cormier, R. Rentelis, A. Schembri, K. Rowley, R. Adam and B. Woll (2014a), *BSL SignBank: A Lexical Database of British Sign Language (1st ed)*. Available online: https://bslsignbank.ucl.ac.uk/ (accessed 15 November 2021).

Fenlon, J., A. Schembri, R. Rentelis, D. Vinson and K. Cormier (2014b), 'Using conversational data to determine lexical frequency in British Sign Language: The influence of text type', *Lingua*, 143: 187–202.

Fenlon, J., K. Cormier and A. Schembri (2015), 'Building BSL Signbank: The lemma dilemma revisited', *International Journal of Lexicography*, 28 (2): 169–206.

Ferrara, L. (2019), 'Coordinating signs and eye gaze in the depiction of directions and spatial scenes by fluent and L2 signers of Norwegian Sign Language', *Spatial Cognition and Computation*, 19 (3): 220–51.

Ferrera, L. (2020), 'Some interactional functions of finger pointing in signed language conversations', *Glossa*, 5 (1): 1–26.

Figueredo, G. (2020), 'Axial argumentation and cryptogrammar in textual grammar: THEME in Brazilian Portuguese', in J. R. Martin, Y. J. Doran and G. Figueredo (eds), *Systemic Functional Language Description: Making Meaning Matter*, 129–61, Oxford: Routledge.

Firbas, J. (1987), 'On the delimitation of the theme in functional sentence perspective', in R. Dirven and V. Fried (eds), *Functionalism in Linguistics*, 137–56, Amsterdam: John Benjamins.

Firth, J. R. (1935), 'The technique of semantics', *Transactions of the Philological Society 1935*, 34 (1): 36–72.

Fontaine, L. (2013), *Analysing English Grammar: A Systemic Functional Introduction*, Cambridge: Cambridge University Press.

Forey, G. and N. Sampson (2017), 'Textual metafunction and theme: What's "it" about?', in T. Bartlett and G. O'Grady (eds), *The Routledge Handbook of Systemic Functional Linguistics*, 131–45, Oxford: Routledge.

Fries, P. H. (2000), 'Issues in modelling the textual metafunction', in M. Scott and G. Thompson (eds), *Patterns of Text: In honour of Michael Hoey*, 83–107, Amsterdam: John Benjamins.

Gabarró-López, S. (2019), 'When the meaning of SAME is not restricted to likeness: A preliminary study from the perspective of discourse relational devices in two sign languages', *Discours*, 24.

Gleason, H. A. (1965), *Linguistics and English Grammar*, New York: Holt, Rinehart and Winston.

Goldin-Meadow, S. and D. Brentari (2017), 'Gesture, sign and language: The coming of age of sign language and gesture studies', *Behavioural and Brain Sciences*, 40 (46): 1–60.

Gwilliams, L. and L. Fontaine (2015), 'Indeterminacy in process type classification', *Functional Linguistics*, 2 (8): 1–19.

Halliday, M. A. K. (1961/2002), 'Categories of the theory of grammar', in J. J. Webster (ed.), *On Grammar: The Collected Works of M. A. K. Halliday (Vol. 1)*, 37–94, London: Continuum.

Halliday, M. A. K. (1967), 'Notes on transitivity and theme in English: Part 2', *Journal of Linguistics*, 3 (2): 199–244.

Halliday, M. A. K. (1975), *Learning How to Mean: Explorations in the Development of Language*, London: Edward Arnold.

Halliday, M. A. K. (1991/2007), 'The notion of "context" in language education', in J. J. Webster (ed.), *Language and Education: The Collected Works of M.A.K. Halliday (Vol. 9)*, 269–90, New York: Bloomsbury Academic.

Halliday, M. A. K. and W. S. Greaves (2008), *Intonation in the Grammar of English*, London: Equinox.

Halliday, M. A. K. and R. Hasan (1976), *Cohesion in English*, Essex: Pearson Education.

Halliday, M. A. K. and C. M. I. M. Matthiessen (1999), *Construing Experience through Meaning: A Language-based Approach to Cognition*, London: Continuum.

Halliday, M. A. K. and C. M. I. M. Matthiessen (2014), *Halliday's Introduction to Functional Grammar*, 4th edn, Oxford: Routledge.

Hanke, T. (2004), 'HamNoSys—Representing sign language data in language resources and language processing contexts', in O. Streiter and C. Vettori (eds), *Fourth International Conference on Language Resources and Evaluation (LREC 2004) Representation and Processing of Sign Languages Workshop*, 1–6, Paris: European Language Resources Association.

Hansen, M. and J. Heßmann (2007), 'Matching propositional content and formal markers Sentence boundaries in a DGS text', *Sign Language & Linguistics*, 10 (2): 145–75.

Hao, J. and S. Hood (2019), 'Valuing science: The role of language and body language in a health science lecture', *Journal of Pragmatics*, 139: 200–15.

Harrison, S. (2018), *The Impulse to Gesture: Where Language, Mind, and Bodies Intersect*, Cambridge: Cambridge University Press.

Hasan, R. (1999), 'Speaking with reference to context', in M. Ghadessy (ed.), *Text and Context in Functional Linguistics*, 219–328, Amsterdam: John Benjamins.

Hasan, R. (2014), 'Towards a paradigmatic description of context: Systems, metafunctions, and semantics', *Functional Linguistics*, 2 (9): 1–54.

Hjelmslev, L. (1963), *Prolegomena to a Theory of Language* (F. J. Whitfield, Trans.), Madison, WI: University of Wisconsin Press (original work published 1943).

Hodge, G. (2013), *Patterns from a Signed Language Corpus: Clause-like Units in Auslan (Australian Sign Language)*, Doctoral thesis, Macquarie University, Sydney.

Hodge, G. and T. Johnston (2014), 'Points, depictions, gestures and enactment: Partly lexical and non-lexical signs as core elements of single clause-like units in Auslan (Australian Sign Language)', *Australian Journal of Linguistics*, 34 (2): 262–91.

Jackson, P. (2001), *A Pictorial History of Deaf Britain*, Cheshire: Deafprint.

Jakobson, R. (1966), 'Implications of language universals for linguistics', in J. H. Greenberg (ed.), *Universals of Language (2nd ed)*, 263–77, Cambridge, MA: MIT Press.

Jantunen, T. (2007), 'The equative sentence in Finnish Sign Language', *Sign Language & Linguistics*, 10 (2): 113–43.

Johnston, T. (1996), 'Function and medium in the forms of linguistic expression found in a sign language', in W. H. Edmondson and R. B. Wilbur (eds), *International Review of Sign Linguistics (Vol. 1)*, 57–94, Mahwah, NJ: Lawrence Erlbaum.

Johnston, T. (2003), 'BSL, Auslan and NZSL: Three signed languages or one?', in A. Baker, B. van den Bogaerde and O. Crasborn (eds), *Cross-linguistic Perspectives in Sign Language Research, Selected Papers from TISLR 2000*, 47–69, Hamburg: Signum Verlag.

Johnston, T. A. (2019), 'Clause constituents, arguments and the question of grammatical relations in Auslan (Australian Sign Language)', *Studies in Language*, 43 (4): 941–96.

Kendon, A. (2004), *Gesture: Visible Action as Utterance*, Cambridge: Cambridge University Press.

Kok, K., K. Bergmann, A. Cienki and S. Kopp (2016), 'Mapping out the multifunctionality of speakers' gestures', *Gesture*, 15 (1): 37–59.

Kress, G. (2010), *Multimodality: A Social Semiotic Approach to Contemporary Communication*, Oxford: Routledge.

Kress, G. and T. van Leeuwen (2006), *Reading Images: The Grammar of Visual Design*, 2nd edn, Oxford: Routledge.

Kusters, A., M. De Meulder and D. O'Brien, eds (2017), *Innovations in Deaf Studies: The Role of Deaf Scholars*, Oxford: Oxford University Press.

Kusters, A. and S. Sahasrabudhe (2018), 'Language ideologies on the difference between gesture and sign', *Language and Communication*, 60: 44–63.

Kusters, A., M. Spotti, R. Swanwick and E. Tapio (2017), 'Beyond languages, beyond modalities: Transforming the study of semiotic repertoires', *International Journal of Multilingualism*, 14 (3), 219–32.

Labov, W. (1972), *Sociolinguistic Patterns*, Philadelphia, PA: University of Pennsylvania Press.

Ladd, P. (2003), *Understanding Deaf Culture – In Search of Deafhood*, Bristol: Multilingual Matters.

LaPolla, R. (2020), 'Arguments for seeing theme-rheme and topic-comment as separate functional structures', in J. R. Martin, Y. J. Doran and G. Figueredo (eds), *Systemic Functional Language Description: Making Meaning Matter*, 162–86, Oxford: Routledge.

Lavid, J., J. Arús and J. R. Zamorano-Mansilla (2010), *Systemic Functional Grammar of Spanish: A Contrastive Study with English*, London: Continuum.

Lawson, L., F. McLean, R. O'Neill and R. Wilks (2019), 'Recognising British Sign Language in Scotland', in M. De Meulder, J. J Murray and R. McKee (eds), *The Legal Recognition of Sign Languages: Advocacy and Outcomes Around the World*, 105–23, Bristol: Multilingual Matters.

Leckie-Tarry, H. (1995), *Language & Context: A Functional Linguistic Theory of Register*, London: Pinter.

Lewin, D. and A. C. Schembri (2011), 'Mouth gestures in British Sign Language: A case study of tongue protrusion in BSL narratives', *Sign Language & Linguistics*, 14 (1): 94–114.

Li, E. S. (2007), *A Systemic Functional Grammar of Chinese*, London: Continuum.

Mandel, M. A. (1981), 'Phonotactics and morphophonology in American Sign Language', Unpublished Doctoral thesis. University of California.

Mapson, R. (2014), 'Polite appearances: How non-manual features convey politeness in British Sign Language', *Journal of Politeness Research*, 10 (2): 157–84.

Mapson, R. (2020), 'Intercultural (Im)politeness: Influences on the way professional British Sign Language/English interpreters mediate im/polite language', in D. Archer, K. Grainger and P. Jagodziński (eds), *Politeness in Professional Contexts*, 151–78, Amsterdam: John Benjamins.

Martin, J. R. (1988), 'Hypotactic recursive systems in English: Towards a functional interpretation', in J. D. Benson and W. S. Greaves (eds), *Systemic Functional Approaches to Discourse*, 240–70, Norwood, NJ: Ablex.

Martin, J. R. (1992), *English Text: System and Structure*, Amsterdam: John Benjamins.

Martin, J. R. (1995), 'Logical meaning, interdependency and the linking particle {-ng/na} in Tagalog', *Functions of Language* 2 (2): 189–228.

Martin, J. R. (2004), 'Positive discourse analysis: Solidarity and change', *Revista Canaria de Estudios Ingleses*, 49 (1): 179–200.

Martin, J. R. (2010), 'Semantic variation – Modelling realisation, instantiation and individuation in social semiosis', in M. Bednarek and J. R. Martin (eds), *New Discourse on Language: Functional Perspectives on Multimodality, Identity and Affiliation*, 1–34, London: Continuum.

Martin, J. R. (2016), 'Meaning matters: A short history of systemic functional linguistics', *Word*, 62 (1): 35–58.

Martin, J. R. (2018), 'Introduction. Interpersonal meaning: Systemic functional linguistics perspective', *Functions of Language*, 25 (1): 2–19.

Martin, J. R. and Y. J. Doran, eds (2015), *Grammatical Descriptions: Volume II in Critical Concepts in Systemic Functional Linguistics*, London: Routledge.

Martin, J. R. and B. Quiroz (2020), 'Functional language typology: A discourse semantic perspective', in J. R. Martin, Y. J. Doran and G. Figueredo (eds), *Systemic Functional Language Description: Making Meaning Matter*, 189–235, London: Routledge.

Martin, J. R. and B. Quiroz (2021), 'Functional language typology: SFL perspectives', in M. Kim, J. Munday, P. Wang and Z. Wang (eds), *Systemic Functional Linguistics in Translation Studies*, 7–33, London: Bloomsbury.

Martin, J. R. and D. Rose (2007), *Working with Discourse: Meaning Beyond the Clause*, 2nd edn, London: Continuum.

Martin, J. R. and D. Rose (2008), *Genre Relations: Mapping Culture*, London: Equinox.

Martin, J. and M. Zappavigna (2019), 'Embodied meaning: A systemic functional perspective on paralanguage', *Functional Linguistics*, 6 (1), 1–33.

Martin, J. R., Y. J. Doran and G. Figueredo, eds (2020), *Systemic Functional Language Description – Making Meaning Matter*, Oxford: Routledge.

Martin, J. R. and P. R. R. White (2005), *The Language of Evaluation: Appraisal in English*, Basingstoke: Palgrave Macmillan.

Martin, J. R., Y. S. Zhu and P. Wang (2013), *Systemic Functional Grammar: A Next Step into the Theory – Axial Relations*, Beijing: Higher Education Press.

Martin, J. R., B. Quiroz and G. Figueredo, eds (2021), *Interpersonal Grammar: Systemic Functional Linguistic Theory and Description*, Cambridge: Cambridge University Press.

Martin, J. R., B. Quiroz, P. Wang and Y. Zhu (2021), *Systemic Functional Grammar: Another Step into the Theory – Grammatical Description*, Beijing: Higher Education Press.

Martinec, R. (2004), 'Gestures that co-occur with speech as a systematic resource: The realization of experiential meanings in indexes', *Social Semiotics*, 14 (2): 193–213.

Martinec, R. (2005), 'Topics in multimodality', in R. Hasan, C. M. I. M. Matthiessen and J. Webster (eds), *Continuing Discourse on Language: A Functional Perspective*, 157–81, London: Equinox.

Mathesius, V. (1939), 'O tak zvaném aktuálním členění větném (On the so-called functional sentence perspective)', *Slovo a Slovesnost*, 5: 171–74.

Matthiessen, C. M. I. M. (1995), *Lexicogrammatical Cartography: English Systems*, Tokyo: International Language Sciences Publishers.

Matthiessen, C. M. I. M. (2004a), 'The evolution of language: A systemic functional exploration of phylogenetic phases', in A. Lukin and G. Williams (eds), *The Development of Language*, 45–90, London: Continuum.

Matthiessen, C. M. I. M. (2004b), 'Descriptive motifs and generalisations', in A. Caffarel, J. R. Martin and C. M. I. M. Matthiessen (eds), *Language Typology: A Functional Perspective*, 537–674, Amsterdam: John Benjamins.

Matthiessen, C. M. I. M. (2009), 'Ideas and new directions', in M. A. K. Halliday and J. J. Webster (eds), *Continuum Companion to Systemic Functional Linguistics*, 12–58, London: Continuum.

Matthiessen, C. M. I. M. (2019), 'Register in systemic functional linguistics', *Register Studies*, 1 (1): 10–41.

Matthiessen, C. M. I. M. and J. A. Bateman (1991), *Text Generation and Systemic-Functional Linguistics: Experiences from English and Japanese*, London: Pinter.

Matthiessen, C. M. I. M., K. Teruya and W. Canzhong (2008), 'Multilingual studies as a multi-dimensional space of interconnected language studies', in J. J. Webster (ed.), *Meaning in Context: Strategies for Implementing Intelligent Applications of Language Studies*, 146–220, London: Continuum.

Matthiessen, C. M. I. M., K. Teruya and M. Lam (2010), *Key Terms in Systemic Functional Linguistics*, London: Continuum.

Malinowski, B. (1923), 'The problem of meaning in primitive languages', in C. K. Ogden and I. A. Richards (eds), *The Meaning of Meaning*, 297–336, London: Kegan Paul.

McKee, R., A. Schembri, D. McKee and T. Johnston (2011), 'Variable "subject" presence in Australian Sign Language and New Zealand Sign Language', *Language Variation and Change*, 23 (3): 375–98.

McKee, R. L. (2001), *People of the Eye: Stories from the Deaf World*, Wellington: Bridget Williams Books.

Moore, E. (2008), 'A lesson from history', *BATOD Magazine*, March: 4–6.

Moore, N. (2016), 'What's the point? The role of punctuation in realising information structure in written English', *Functional Linguistics*, 3 (6): 1–23.

Müller, C. (2018), 'Gesture and sign: Cataclysmic break or dynamic relations?' *Frontiers in Psychology*, 9 (1651): 1–20.

Mwinlaaru, I. N. and W. W. Xuan (2016), 'A survey of studies in systemic functional language description and typology', *Functional Linguistics*, 3 (8): 1–41.

Napier, J. and L. Leeson (2016), *Sign Language in Action*, London: Palgrave Macmillan.

Napoli, D. J. and R. Sutton-Spence (2014), 'Order of the major constituents in sign languages: Implications for all language', *Frontiers in Psychology*, 5: 1–18.

Neidle, C., J. Kegl, D. MacLaughlin, B. Bahan and R. G. Lee (2000), *The Syntax of American Sign Language: Functional Categories and Hierarchical Structure*, Cambridge, MA: MIT Press.

Ngo, T., J. R. Martin, C. Painter, B. Smith and M. Zappavigna (2021), *Modelling Paralanguage Using Systemic Functional Semiotics*, London: Bloomsbury.

Office for National Statistics (2013), *2011 Census: Detailed Analysis – English Language Proficiency in England and Wales*, Main language and general health characteristics. Available online: https://www.ons.gov.uk/peoplepopulationandcommunity/culturalidentity/language/articles/detailedanalysisenglishlanguageproficiencyinenglandandwales/2013-08-30 (accessed 15 November 2021).

O'Grady, G. (2017), 'Intonation and systemic functional linguistics: The way forward', in T. Bartlett and. G. O'Grady (eds), *The Routledge Handbook of Systemic Functional Linguistics*, 146–62, Oxford: Routledge.

Orfanidou, E., R. Adam, J. M. McQueen and G. Morgan (2009), 'Making sense of nonsense in British Sign Language (BSL): The contribution of different phonological parameters to sign recognition', *Memory & Cognition*, 37 (3): 302–15.

Padden, C. A. (2015), 'Methods of research on sign language grammars', in E. Orfanidou, B. Woll and G. Morgan (eds), *Research Methods in Sign Language Studies*, 143–55, Sussex: Wiley Blackwell.

Painter, C. (1989), *Learning the Mother Tongue*, Oxford: Oxford University Press.

Painter, C. (2015), *Into the Mother Tongue*, London: Bloomsbury Academic.

Perniss, P., A. Özyürek and G. Morgan (2015), 'The influence of the visual modality on language structure and conventionalization: Insights from sign language and gesture', *Topics in Cognitive Science*, 7 (1): 2–11.

Peterson, M. A. and B. S. Gibson (1994), 'Object recognition contributions to figure-ground organization: Operations on outlines and subjective contours', *Perception & Psychophysics*, 56: 551–64.

Pfau, R. and H. Bos (2016), 'Syntax: Simple sentences', in A. Baker, B. van den Bogaerde, R. Pfau and T. Schermer (eds), *The Linguistics of Sign Languages: An Introduction*, 117–48, Amsterdam: John Benjamins.

Pike, Kenneth L. (1982), *Linguistic Concepts: An Introduction to Tagmemics*, Lincoln, NE: University of Nebraska Press.

Quinn, G. (2010), 'Schoolization: An account of the origins of regional variation in British Sign Language', *Sign Language Studies*, 10 (4): 476–501.

Quiroz, B. (2018), 'Negotiating interpersonal meanings', *Functions of Language*, 25 (1): 135–63.

Quiroz, B. (2020), 'Experiential cryptotypes: Reasoning about PROCESSS TYPE', in J. R. Martin, Y. J. Doran and G. Figueredo (eds), *Systemic Functional Language Description: Making Meaning Matter*, 102–28, Oxford: Routledge.

Rathkey, E. S. (2019), *Can ASL-Gloss be Used as an Instructional Tool to Teach Written English to the Deaf?* Doctoral thesis. Kingston, RI: The University of Rhode Island.

Reagan, T. (2019), *Linguistic Legitimacy and Social Justice*, Cham: Palgrave Macmillan.

Rose, D. (2007), 'Reading genre: A new wave of analysis', *Linguistics and the Human Sciences*, 2 (2): 185–204.

Rose, D. and J. R. Martin (2012), *Learning to Write, Reading to Learn: Genre, Knowledge and Pedagogy in the Sydney School*, London: Equinox.

Royal Association for Deaf People (2020), *What Is British Sign Language?* Available online: https://www.royaldeaf.org.uk/about-us/what-is-bsl/ (accessed 15 November 2021).

Rudge, L. A. (2015), 'Towards an understanding of contextual features that influence the linguistic formality of British Sign Language users', *Functional Linguistics*, 2 (11): 1–17.

Rudge, L. A. (2018), *Analysing British Sign Language through the lens of Systemic Functional Linguistics*. Doctoral thesis. Bristol: University of the West of England.

Rudge, L. A. (2020), 'Situating simultaneity: An initial schematisation of the lexicogrammatical rank scale of British Sign Language', *Word*, 66 (2): 98–118.

Rudge, L. A. (2021), 'Interpersonal grammar in British Sign Language', in J. R. Martin, B. Quiroz and G. Figueredo (eds), *Interpersonal Grammar: Systemic Functional Linguistic Theory and Description*, 227–56, Cambridge: Cambridge University Press.

Sandler, W. (1999), 'The medium and the message: Prosodic interpretation of linguistic content in Israeli Sign Language', *Sign Language and Linguistics*, 2 (2): 187–215.

Sandler, W. and D. Lillo-Martin (2006), *Sign Language and Linguistic Universals*, Cambridge: Cambridge University Press.

Schembri, A. and C. Lucas, eds (2015), *Sociolinguistics and Deaf Communities*, Cambridge: Cambridge University Press.

Selleck, C. L. (2017), 'Ethnographic chats: A best of both method for ethnography', *Sky Journal of Linguistics*, 30: 151–62.

Shintel, H. and H. C. Nusbaum (2007), 'The sound of motion in language: Visual information conveyed by acoustic properties of speech', *Cognition*, 105 (3): 681–90.

Sicard, R. A. (1984), 'Course of instruction for a congenitally deaf person', in H. Lane and F. Philip (eds), *The Deaf Experience: Classics in Language and Education*, 81–126, London: Harvard University Press.

Slobin, D. I., N. Hoiting, M. Anthony, Y. Biederman, M. Kuntze, R. Lindert, J. Pyers, H. Thumann and A. Weinberg (2001) 'Sign language transcription at the level of meaning components: The Berkeley Transcription System (BTS)', *Sign Language & Linguistics*, 4 (1–2): 63–104.

Stamp, R., A. Schembri, J. Fenlon, R. Rentelis, B. Woll and K. Cormier (2014), 'Lexical variation and change in British Sign Language', *PLoS ONE*, 9 (4): 811–24.

Stamp, R., A. Schembri, J. Fenlon and R. Rentelis (2015), 'Sociolinguistic variation and change of British Sign Language number signs', *Sign Language Studies*, 15 (2): 151–81.

Stewart-Taylor, L. (2021), *Where Is the Interpreter?* Available online: https://www.whereistheinterpreter.com (accessed 15 November 2021).

Stokoe, W. C. (1960), *Sign Language Structure*, Silver Spring, MD: Linstok Press.

Sutton-Spence, R. (1999), 'The influence of English on British Sign Language', *International Journal of Bilingualism*, 3 (4): 363–94.

Sutton-Spence, R. and B. Woll (1999), *The Linguistics of British Sign Language: An Introduction*, Cambridge: Cambridge University Press.

Tallerman, M. (2015), *Understanding Syntax*, 4th edn, Oxford: Routledge.

Tann, K. (2017), 'Context and meaning in the Sydney architecture of systemic functional linguistics', in T. Bartlett and G. O'Grady (eds), *The Routledge Handbook of Systemic Functional Linguistics*, 438–56, Oxford: Routledge.

Taverniers, M. (2011), 'The syntax-semantics interface in systemic functional grammar: Halliday's interpretation of the Hjelmslevian model of stratification', *Journal of Pragmatics*, 43 (4): 1100–26.

Teruya, K. (2007), *A Systemic Functional Grammar of Japanese*, Vol 1 and 2, London: Continuum.

Tervoort, B. T. M. (1953), *Structurele analyse van visueel taalgebruik binnen een groep dove kinderen*. Doctoral thesis. Amsterdam: University of Amsterdam.

Thomson, E. A., P. R. R. White and P. Kitley (2008), '"Objectivity" and "hard news" reporting across cultures: Comparing the news report in English, French, Japanese and Indonesian journalism', *Journalism Studies*, 9 (2): 212–28.

Torsello, C. (1996), 'On the logical metafunction', *Functions of Language*, 3 (2): 151–83.

van der Kooij, E. and O. Crasborn (2016), 'Phonology', in A. Baker, B. van den
    Bogaerde, R. Pfau and T. Schermer (eds), *The Linguistics of Sign Languages: An
    Introduction*, 251–78, Amsterdam: John Benjamins.

van Leeuwen, T. (2008), *Discourse and Practice – New Tools for Critical Discourse
    Analysis*, Oxford: Oxford University Press.

Ventola, E. (1987), *The Structure of Social Interaction: A Systemic Approach to the
    Semiotics of Service Encounters*, London: Pinter.

Volterra, V., A. Laudanna, S. Corazza, E. Radutzky and F. Natale (1984), 'Italian Sign
    Language: The order of elements in the declarative sentence', in F. Loncke, P. Boyes
    Braem and Y. Lebrun (eds), *Recent Research on European Sign Languages*, 19–46,
    Lisse: Swets and Zeitlinger BV.

Wang, P. (2020), 'Axial argumentation and cryptogrammar in interpersonal grammar: A
    case study of classical Tibetan MOOD', in J. R. Martin, Y. J. Doran and G. Figueredo
    (eds), *Systemic Functional Language Description: Making Meaning Matter*, 73–101,
    Oxford: Routledge.

Whorf, B. L. (1945). 'Grammatical categories', *Language*, 21 (1): 1–11.

Wille, B., K. Mouvet, M. Vermeerbergen and M. van Herreweghe (2018), 'Flemish Sign
    Language – A case study on deaf mother – deaf child interactions', *Functions of
    Language*, 25 (2): 289–322.

Woodward, J. (1975), 'How you gonna get to heaven if you can't talk with Jesus: The
    educational establishment vs. the deaf community', *Paper Presented at the 34th
    Annual Meeting of the Society for Applied Anthropology*, Amsterdam.

World Federation of the Deaf (2014), *WFD Statement on Sign Language Work*, Helsinki:
    World Federation of the Deaf. Available online: http://wfdeaf.org/wp-content/
    uploads/2016/11/WFD-statement-sign-language-work.pdf (accessed 15 November
    2021).

Yule, D. (2014), *The Study of Language*, 5th edn, Cambridge: Cambridge University
    Press.

Zeshan, U. (2000), *Sign Language in Indo-Pakistan: A Description of a Signed Language*,
    Amsterdam: John Benjamins.

Index

American Sign Language (ASL) 4
Australian Sign Language (Auslan) 6, 13,
  18, 31–2, 107, 145, 150, 152

British Sign Language (BSL)
  British, Australian and New Zealand
    Sign Language (BANZSL) 6
  classifier construction. *See* depicting
    construction.
  constructed action 34, 80, 143
  depicting construction 14, 26, 34,
    79–80, 154 n.3
  legal recognition 5, 147, 152
  negation 56–7, 115
  number of users 4–5
  politeness 29–30
  primary systems
    CIRCUMSTANCE 93–6, 128
    CLAUSE FOCUS 114–18, 128, 136, 151
    MODALITY 58–62, 69, 128, 131,
      139–40, 148
    MOOD 43–52, 68–9, 109, 115, 128,
      131, 133, 139, 148
    MULTIPLE THEME 110–11, 128, 134,
      136, 139, 143
    POLARITY 52–8, 69, 128, 131, 139,
      148–9
    PROCESS TYPE 75–93, 109, 128, 134,
      142, 149
    SOCIAL PROXIMITY 62–5, 69, 128, 149
    THEME ELLIPSIS 111–14, 128, 134,
      136
  role shift. *See* constructed action.
  tone 47, 111, 133, 136

Catalan Sign Language. *See* llengua de
  signes catalana (LSC).
Chilean Spanish 29, 47, 49
circumstances 93–6, 134, 138, 149
clause
  clause-like unit (CLU) 31–2, 147
  identification 30–4
  as rank 23, 27–8

context 19–20, 22–3, 126
contextual parameters
  field 22, 72–3, 102
  mode 22, 102–3
  tenor 21–2, 40–1, 102–3

deaf
  or Deaf 2
  educational provision 5
  studies 4–7, 146–7
Deutsche Gebärdensprache (DGS) 31
discourse semantics
  as stratum 19, 29, 126
  systems
    APPRAISAL 110, 151
    IDEATION 73–5
    IDENTIFICATION 103
    NEGOTIATION 41
    PERIODICITY 104
    SPEECH FUNCTION 40–2, 45–6, 110
    TRACKING 103
domains of experience 73–5

ergativity 75, 149
EUDICO Linguistic Annotator (ELAN)
  32–3

Finnish Sign Language (FinSL). *See*
  suomalainen viittomakieli.
Flemish Sign Language 18, 152
French Belgian Sign Language. *See*
  Langue des signes de Belgique
  francophone (LSFB).

German Sign Language. *See* Deutsche
  Gebärdensprache (DGS).
gesture
  co-speech 17, 35–7, 152
  distinction from sign languages 36–7
  mouth 9, 13
  and paralanguage 17
Given-New 105–7, 116–18, 122, 136, 143
grammatical metaphor 140

www.ingramcontent.com/pod-product-compliance
Lightning Source LLC
Chambersburg PA
CBHW050515280326
41932CB00014B/2334